IN THE
SHADOW OF
THE DEBT

IN THE SHADOW OF THE DEBT

Emerging Issues in Latin America

Robert Bottome
Roberto Bouzas
Benjamin J. Cohen
Anatole Kaletsky

Marcílio Marques Moreira
Felipe Ortiz de Zevallos M.
Luis Rubio
Arturo Valenzuela

The Twentieth Century Fund Press/New York/1992

The Twentieth Century Fund is a research foundation undertaking timely analyses of economic, political, and social issues. Not-for-profit and non-partisan, the Fund was founded in 1919 and endowed by Edward A. Filene.

BOARD OF TRUSTEES OF THE TWENTIETH CENTURY FUND

Morris B. Abram, Emeritus
H. Brandt Ayers
Peter A. A. Berle
José A. Cabranes
Joseph A. Califano, Jr.
Alexander Morgan Capron
Edward E. David, Jr.
Brewster C. Denny, *Chairman*
Charles V. Hamilton
August Heckscher, Emeritus
Matina S. Horner
Madeleine M. Kunin

James A. Leach
Richard C. Leone, ex officio
Georges-Henri Martin, Emeritus
P. Michael Pitfield
Don K. Price, Emeritus
Richard Ravitch
Arthur M. Schlesinger, Jr., Emeritus
Harvey I. Sloane, M.D.
Theodore C. Sorensen
James Tobin, Emeritus
David B. Truman, Emeritus
Shirley Williams

Richard C. Leone, *President*

Library of Congress Cataloging-in-Publication Data

In the shadow of the debt: emerging issues in Latin America/Robert Bottome ... [et al.].
    p.   cm.
  Includes bibliographical references.
  ISBN 0-87078-339-4 : $10.95
  1. Latin America—Economic conditions—1982- 2. Debts, External—Latin America. 3. Latin America—Politics and government—1980-
I. Bottome, Robert.
HC125.I363 1992   92-5469
336.3'435'098—dc20   CIP

Copyright © 1992 by the Twentieth Century Fund, Inc.
Manufactured in the United States of America.

Foreword

We are about to mark the tenth anniversary of the international debt crisis. In August 1982, Mexico failed to meet payments on its commercial bank loans, setting off a spiral of debt rescheduling and near defaults in Latin America and prompting fears in the United States and elsewhere that the international banking system would collapse. A decade later, the Mexican economy is growing at over 4 percent annually; debt has ceased to be a major issue in Mexican politics; and the United States, Canada, and Mexico are negotiating a North American Free Trade Agreement (NAFTA).

Mexico's path from precipitator of the debt crisis to paragon of economic reform is only one of a number of dramatic transformations that occurred in the Western Hemisphere in the past ten years. The 1980s may have been a "lost decade" for Latin America in terms of economic growth, but they also marked the transition from military to civilian rule in Chile, Argentina, Brazil, and many other countries, as well as the adoption of significant economic reform measures across the region.

While democratization and economic reform are the rule throughout Latin America, differences among individual countries remain extremely important. In some countries, democratization has complicated the task of economic reform; in others, it has brought a move toward even greater political opening; and, of course, the speed and success of economic reform has varied from country to country. But one trend is clear: the altered political and economic landscape of Latin America, reinforced by the end of the cold war and growing U.S. preoccupation with issues closer to home, has cleared the way for an unprecedented degree of hemispheric collaboration. Among the issues now on the inter-American agenda, in addition to the NAFTA negotiations, are the Enterprise for the Americas Initiative announced by the Bush administration in June 1990, the establishment of a four-country common market in the Southern Cone (MERCOSUR), and discussion of hemispheric trade arrangements that might go beyond North America.

Closer cooperation between the United States and Latin America is also possible because, to a large degree, the issue that dominated hemispheric relations throughout the 1980s—the debt crisis—has receded as a focus of attention in North and South alike. For many countries, debt remains an issue. But other concerns are emerging from its shadows. In some cases, these are new questions; in others, they were there all along, obscured by the overriding focus on debt. Restructuring the economy, attracting foreign investment, seeking new trade opportunities, privatizing industry, and safeguarding the environment are among the challenges now facing many Latin American governments.

Between 1984 and 1989, the Twentieth Century published a series of papers on the international debt crisis. Written in the years immediately following its onset, they addressed the root causes and possible resolution of the crisis in individual countries. Among these were *The Brazilian Quandary* by Marcílio Marques Moreira, *The Peruvian Puzzle* by Felipe Ortiz de Zevallos, and *A Mexican Response*, coauthored by Luis Rubio. The series included several papers on broader topics, including *The Costs of Default* by Anatole Kaletsky, and culminated in *The Road to Economic Recovery*, the Report of the Twentieth Century Fund Task Force on International Debt.

In the Shadow of the Debt: Emerging Issues in Latin America returns to many of the issues raised by the earlier series. Our interest in this subject is part of the Fund's continuing focus on hemispheric economic and trade issues. Michelle Miller, Vice President for Programs, is directing our ongoing work in this area. In addition to essays by Kaletsky, Marques Moreira, Ortiz de Zevallos, and Rubio, this volume contains chapters on Argentina, Chile, and Venezuela, as well as an analysis of U.S. government policy toward the debt crisis. As managing the problem of third world debt recedes in importance to U.S. policy and other issues emerge from its shadows, this volume presents the concerns of Latin Americans to a U.S. audience. We hope that these essays will help inform the thinking of policymakers in the United States and Canada about the hemisphere we share.

Richard C. Leone, *President*
The Twentieth Century Fund
March 1992

Contents

Foreword *by Richard C. Leone*	v
1 / Introduction *by Anatole Kaletsky*	1
2 / Political and Economic Challenges for Chile's Transition to Democracy *by Arturo Valenzuela*	13
3 / Solving the Peruvian Puzzle *by Felipe Ortiz de Zevallos M.*	37
4 / Venezuela: The Struggle for Reform *by Robert Bottome*	59
5 / Beyond Stabilization and Reform: The Argentine Economy in the 1990s *by Roberto Bouzas*	83
6 / Mexico: Debt and Reform *by Luis Rubio*	111
7 / The Brazilian Quandary Revisited *by Marcílio Marques Moreira*	129
8 / U.S. Debt Policy in Latin America: The Melody Lingers on *by Benjamin J. Cohen*	153
About the Authors	173

1 / Introduction

Anatole Kaletsky

The decade that followed the Mexican debt default of August 1982 was the worst in the modern history of Latin America. It was also the best.

This is the curious message of almost every essay in this collection. In terms of the statistical indicators of economic development, the ten years from 1982 to 1991 were indeed a "lost decade," as Latin Americans have lamented from Mexico City to Santiago. Yet, far from provoking the violent social upheavals or neofascist coups that were so widely predicted during the throes of the economic depression, the 1980s saw a flowering of democracy, an opening up to the outside world, and a revival of competitive capitalism of a kind not seen in Latin America since World War II. This concatenation of economic disaster with political progress in Latin America has been one of the most important and unexpected historical developments of the late twentieth century.

Although it has been overshadowed in the public mind and the attention of policymakers by the collapse of communism in Eastern Europe, the transformation of Latin America in the 1980s has had many features in common with the lifting of the iron curtain. And its worldwide implications could turn out to be almost as broad. Just as the paralysis and implosion of the Communist economic superstructure turned out to be the critical condition for the overthrow of the entire totalitarian system in Europe, so in Latin America the rejection of populist-authoritarian politics, with military overtones, went hand in hand with the collapse of the nationalist-statist economic model.

Given the apparent triumph of Western ideas that coincided with the economic crises in both Eastern Europe and Latin America, it is tempting to infer a causal connection and thereby claim retrospective justification for U.S. diplomatic and financial policies in the 1980s.

President Reagan was roundly criticized and even derided for starting a wasteful arms race against the Soviet Union in 1981. In purely military terms the critics may well have been justified. Many of the hugely expensive weapons programs launched in the 1980s have been scrapped and abandoned even before they are operational. Yet politically, the Reagan defence buildup has been judged by many to be an astounding success. By 1989, President Reagan's arms race was widely given credit for forcing the Communist system into bankruptcy, exposing that bankruptcy even to the system's committed supporters in the military-industrial complex, and thereby sweeping away the fundamental obstacles to reform. A similar retrospective justification might be claimed for Washington's unyielding financial policies after the debt crisis of 1982.

The U.S. government refused to contemplate debt relief, and it insisted, through the International Monetary Fund (IMF), on full interest payments as the sine qua non of every economic rehabilitation program. These policies were lambasted by European, Latin American, and U.S. observers for being financially unrealistic and economically shortsighted.

In this instance, the critics on the economic side won the day. Events confounded the bank and official economists who argued from 1982 until around 1985 that Latin America was suffering from a mere "liquidity problem" and that most countries would restore their creditworthiness after a few years of belt tightening overseen by the IMF. In fact, not one major debtor country proved capable of servicing its full obligations or restoring its creditworthiness before the Brady plan officially sanctioned debt forgiveness in 1989. Even the showcase economies like Chile and Colombia eventually won substantial debt relief through debt-equity swaps and other Brady plan arrangements. The international community's response to the debt crisis (a response that was virtually dictated by the Reagan administration, as Benjamin J. Cohen explains in his contribution to this volume) precipitated a continentwide depression as deep and long as the gloomiest critics had expected.

However, the political impact of this economic disaster was remarkably benign. The depression of the mid-1980s turned out to be the deathblow for the militarism, populism, and mutual distrust among states that had dominated Latin American politics for generations. In retrospect, the debt crisis seems to have been an inadvertent catalyst for the abandonment of protectionist and statist economic ideologies across Latin America. At the administrative level, the failure of the established government bureaucracies to find any way out of the post-1982 economic crises led to a generational shift in the locus of power. The pendulum swung away from the old military-nationalist elites whose politics was built on the economic foundations of the protected industrial monopolies and semifeudal agricultural fiefdoms. Crisis by crisis, a new generation of economic technocrats (many of them educated in the United States) came into ascendance. The reforming technocracy was usually allied to the rising middle class, the financial sectors, and the aspiring industrial exporters—groups that had more to gain than to fear from greater competition and openness to world markets. Ideologically, the liberal technocrats represented a more democratic, as well as a more internationalist, outlook.

As Luis Rubio notes in his essay on Mexico, the new policies were made possible by "a clear political calculation that the 'old order' was politically and socially unsustainable. The reformers recognized that Mexico could not remain aloof from events in the rest of the world and that economic stagnation would eventually destroy the traditional political system."

Looking back over the liberalization of Latin America in the 1980s, it can be argued that the political gains of the decade outweighed the economic losses. It is certainly clear that the political disaster scenarios widely discussed at the height of the debt crisis have not come to pass. There have been few bloody social conflicts traceable to the debt crisis, no anti-American revolutions, and no mass population movements across the Rio Grande. The comments of Felipe Ortiz de Zevallos in his chapter on Peru could be repeated about almost every Latin American country: "Just a quick look [at the economic and social indicators] suggests the possibility of a military coup, impending civil war, or Communist revolution...[but] a new society is emerging in response to the crisis."

But do the encouraging signs of political liberalization and economic rehabilitation in much of Latin America imply that the policies of the United States and other leading industrialized countries in the region have been justified by events? The answer must be a clear no. The unexpected political progress in Latin America has in no way vindicated the U.S. approach to the Western Hemisphere's crisis of debt and development. This answer is of more than historic interest because important parts of the economic philosophy that dominated Western Hemisphere relations in the 1980s continue to shape the economic diplomacy of the 1990s and have spread their influence beyond Latin America. Yet the experience of the 1980s suggests that a very different emphasis is needed in U.S. relations not only with Latin America but also with other developing countries and the ex-Communist world.

There are several reasons why the Latin American strategy of the 1980s must be judged a comprehensive failure. First, it must be recognized that the political breakthroughs in Latin America have not yet been matched by economic recovery, or even stability, in many countries, even a full ten years after the 1982 debt crisis.

While Mexico and Chile now seem to be well on the way to economic growth and development, the same cannot be said of Brazil, Argentina, Venezuela, Peru, or many of Latin America's other countries. As the following chapters on individual countries show, there are hopeful signs almost everywhere, but tangible evidence of economic success is still very limited, especially in Brazil, the region's biggest country and dominant economy. Even in Mexico and Chile, severe economic imbalances persist and confidence in the future remains fragile. In Mexico, gross domestic product is still growing by only 4 percent annually, while the current account deficit is widening again, albeit on the basis of apparently secure inflows of private direct investment from multinationals rather than short-term lending from commercial banks. For Mexico, 4 percent growth represents a disappointing rate of progress, given a population expanding by 2 percent annually and a long-term average of 6 percent growth annually in the decades before 1982. In Chile, too, there are still economic worries as inflation accelerates while export growth slows. Meanwhile, in Argentina, the process of economic rehabilitation is only just beginning. In Brazil, even preliminary signs of stabilization are still nonexistent, despite five crash programs against hyperinflation and two currency reforms.

After ten years of continuously declining real incomes and IMF-monitored adjustment programs across the length and breadth of Latin America, this record gives no cause for complacency. Compared with the conventional forecasts made in the years immediately after the debt crisis, Latin American countries have almost all underperformed by spectacular margins, despite the unexpectedly strong growth of the world economy since then and the debt relief that gradually became available from 1985 onward.[1] From a macroeconomic standpoint, therefore, the debt strategy of the 1980s unambiguously failed.

The philosophy of economic adjustment behind the IMF's stabilization programs has been decisively refuted by the experience in Latin America. Two central tenets of this philosophy, in particular, have been empirically disproved: the idea that controlling domestic inflation is either necessary or sufficient for stabilizing the balance of payments; and the idea that inflation and fiscal deficits are purely macroeconomic problems that can be tackled by macroeconomic means. The U.S. administration and the international financial community would do well to draw the appropriate lessons from the mistakes made in dealing with Latin America.

As Pedro Aspe, the Mexican finance minister, argued forcefully in his 1992 Robbins Lectures, Latin America's experience has shown that macroeconomic stabilization can be successful only if it goes hand in hand with structural change and some measure of debt relief.[2] Attempts to stop inflation, stabilize the currency, or correct the balance of payments before tackling fundamental structural problems of government spending, privatization, wage indexation, and tax collection have invariably failed; they have in fact usually been counterproductive because they undermined confidence in economic management. Latin American economists and politicians argued throughout the 1980s for a reversal of the high priority attached to macroeconomic "adjustment" as opposed to structural reforms. The rehabilitation plans demanded by the IMF and the U.S. government should have put more stress on privatization, tax collection, trade liberalization, and other structural measures, and less on the speedy reduction of current account deficits.

But such arguments have led to another objection to the traditional adjustment philosophy of the IMF. The servicing of an arbitrary level of debt cannot be taken for granted in designing a stabilization program. In one case after another, it has been shown that fully servicing preexisting debts was incompatible with economic stabilization. Debt could be serviced in full, but then inflation would accelerate; or inflation could be controlled, but then part of the debt would have to be forgiven. In Mexico's case, a permanent stabilization program compatible with economic growth only became feasible from 1989 onward, when the Brady plan officially sanctioned significant debt forgiveness.

The general implication is clear, and in the coming months it may need to be applied to Russia and other ex-Communist countries. Neither macroeconomic shock treatment, nor structural reform, nor debt forgiveness is sufficient to stabilize a deeply indebted economy and put it back on a sustainable growth path. What is required is a unified program that implements all three policies in a carefully phased sequence. In designing such a stabilization program, the amount of money to be devoted to debt servicing cannot be set exogenously by the demands of banks and creditor governments. The structure of the economy must determine how much debt servicing is sustainable. If the contractual level of debt is higher than the level compatible with economic stabilization, the excess must be forgiven or deferred. In the language used repeatedly by Latin American leaders but officially repudiated in Washington until the U-turn of 1989, debt service must be determined by ability to pay, not by contractual liability.

While the principle of debt forgiveness has gradually crept into the policies of the IMF and the U.S. administration, it has never been fully acknowledged. Even the Brady plan, which effectively mandated debt forgiveness of 40 percent and upward, was built around the fiction of voluntary agreements between debtor countries and commercial banks. The U.S. government's devotion to such fictions has been a fundamental flaw in its relationship with Latin America.

It was clear from the early stages of the debt crisis that much of Latin America's debt would be written off and forgiven, not only because of economic necessity but also because the commercial balance of power favored the debtors, rather than the creditor governments and banks. The main question was not whether debts would be honored in full, but whether the inevitable debt relief would be arranged by the United States and other creditor governments or seized by the debtors through a series of "conciliatory defaults." (The much-discussed debtors' cartels to present a united front against creditors never appeared plausible and did not, in fact, occur.)

In the end, the process of tacitly acknowledging debt relief took much longer than rational behavior by either the debtors or the creditor governments would have dictated. Relief was arranged through a muddled sequence of conciliatory defaults followed by U.S. government initiatives, culminating in the Brady plan of 1989. In it, Secretary of the Treasury Brady explicitly mentioned the need for debt forgiveness for the first time. In fact, substantial forgiveness had already taken place by that time through debt-equity swaps, buybacks in the secondary market, and other officially encouraged techniques (although the term debt forgiveness was still banned from the official vocabulary a few months before Brady's initiative).

However, Washington's refusal formally to acknowledge the need for debt forgiveness did enormous damage not only to the Latin American countries but also, ironically, to the U.S. economy and banks. Cohen notes that the protection of U.S. banks was always a higher priority for Washington than the maintenance of economic stability in Latin America. This ordering of priorities was dubious politically. Less obviously, it was almost comically counterproductive, even from the narrow perspective of U.S. financial and economic self-interest.

Far from protecting the integrity of the banking system, the behavior of the Federal Reserve (the Fed) and the Treasury actually encouraged the further debasement of U.S. credit standards. The authorities knowingly encouraged false accounting with regard to the realizable value of Latin American loans, connived with the banks to propagate fictions about the legal enforceability of sovereign debt contracts, and actively discouraged the minority of prudent bankers who were inclined to make adequate provisions for their losses. The fear among regulators was that precautionary action by some well-capitalized banks might expose weaker and less prudent institutions to unfavorable comparisons. Worse still, the Fed and the Reagan administration allowed the interests of the banks to dominate their debt strategy, without even requiring the quid pro quos that had previously been common practice in bankruptcies and government financial bailouts: the banks were not required to dismiss their senior managements, to cut their dividends, or to dilute the interest of their existing shareholders by raising new equity. On the contrary, some of the most exposed institutions were allowed to increase dividends and engage in creative accounting to disguise the inevitable costs of debt write-offs.

As a result, two precedents were established: senior executives were not held accountable for the imprudent lending decisions made under their watch; and bank shareholders were insulated for years from making any contribution to the costs of financial reconstruction (though they did ultimately pay a considerable price). Not surprisingly, the U.S. banking industry responded to the new permissiveness with entrepreneurial vigor; the indulgent treatment of bank managements and shareholders after the debt crisis encouraged further waves of reckless lending—the real estate and takeover manias of the mid-to-late 1980s. These frenzies in turn posed greater threats to the U.S. financial system than the debt crisis, as well as requiring bigger government bailouts and doing far more damage to the structure of the U.S. economy.

In addition to fostering a culture of financial irresponsibility on Wall Street, the U.S. government's policies toward Latin America in the 1980s did more direct damage to U.S. industry and trade. The ten years of depression in Latin America have obviously caused severe losses for multinational investors in the region. The decline in Latin America's imports from $101 billion in 1981 to $60 billion in 1983 had still not been made up for by 1990. U.S. manufacturers bore the brunt of this adjustment. The total cost to the U.S. economy of the collapse in trade and investment opportunities in Latin America was probably comparable to the financial losses eventually borne by bank shareholders. But if banks had been forced to accept these losses and the idea of debt forgiveness earlier, the Western Hemisphere's recession could have been much shorter and shallower. The investment and trading losses for the United States and other industrialized countries would have been correspondingly lessened.

A final reason for skepticism about the record of U.S. and other creditor countries' policy toward Latin America comes back to the divergence between the region's political and economic trends. Perhaps a severe economic slump was a price worth paying to demonstrate that "the 'old order' was politically and socially unsustainable," to quote Rubio again. But two further questions arise. Was it necessary to suffer ten years of depression to bankrupt and discredit the "old order" in Latin America? And if so, what does this imply for the region's future and its relationship with the United States and the rest of the world?

The liberalization in Latin America was part of a similar trend around the world. The late 1980s saw remarkable moves in the direction of political and economic liberalism in countries as far-flung as South Korea, India, and South Africa, as well as Eastern Europe. It is quite possible that parts of Latin America would have been carried along by this trend even in the absence of economic crisis. While in Mexico, Argentina, and Brazil, the economic collapse undoubtedly weakened the traditional military and populist power centers, in other countries, such as Chile, the economic crisis gave the military additional excuses for repression. In Chile, it was the rehabilitation of the economy, rather than its collapse, that catalyzed the transition from dictatorship to democracy.

In fact, most Latin Americans believe that the economic crisis has greatly impeded the continent's progress toward democracy and economic liberalism, not encouraged it. Brazilians, for example, widely blame the threat of hyperinflation and depression for making their country ungovernable under its new democratic constitution. Economic stability, they believe, would produce political stability and strengthen democratic institutions. There is, however, a powerful counterargument. In many countries, the military had been expected to take advantage of the economic chaos engendered by the debt crisis to restore the old elites to political dominance. If it failed to do so, this was partly because the officers could see no way out of the economic morass, least of all by applying the time-tested methods of ruthless repression. Had it not been for the depth and duration of the economic crisis, therefore, it is quite possible that the traditional ruling classes would have reasserted themselves in some countries after a brief flowering of democracy in the 1980s.

It is impossible to say definitively whether the economic collapse of the 1980s assisted the Western Hemisphere's progress toward democracy or obstructed it. But let us assume a severe and prolonged economic crisis was necessary in Latin America to overcome the entrenched opposition to reform, just as it was in the Communist world. This assumption has profound implications for Latin America's future and its relationship with the United States and the rest of the world. The United States and the IMF may have inadvertently helped the Latin American polity in the 1980s by destroying its traditional economy. But even if this were true, the unexpectedly benign interaction between the economy and the political system would break down at some point.

While an economic crisis may be necessary to start a political transformation, continuing economic disruption will undermine the foundations of any new political structure once it is in place. The whole of Latin America has now reached the point in its march to democracy where political stability and consolidation are needed. In almost every country, nascent democratic systems have been precariously established, but antidemocratic and xenophobic forces remain powerful and are looking for the chance to reassert themselves.

History suggests that, under such circumstances, the countries that break out of economic depression into sustainable growth have an excellent chance of developing robust democracies, cohesive societies, and productive economies. But those whose economies remain stagnant will be threatened by antidemocratic counterrevolutions. For such countries, the moment of greatest danger may come not at the peak of a hyperinflation nor in the depths of a recession, but during a period of drift in between. For the antidemocratic forces, the opportunity to strike comes when fears of impending catastrophe have abated but hopes of prosperity remain dim.

Latin America has now entered such a period. The decade of depression is over, but the years ahead hold too little hope. If the trends and policies of the past few years are merely projected forward, there can be no firm basis for optimism about the region's prospects. Even in the most successful countries, such as Mexico and Chile, the economic achievements are still tenuous and the financial pressures remain intense. In other countries, including the region's largest, Brazil, the hard work of economic stabilization, privatization, and structural reform has only just begun and the external debt burden has not yet been lifted. The poorest countries—Bolivia, Peru, and the Central American states—have made impressive strides in democratization but remain vulnerable to economic and political shocks that could throw them back into chaos.

Meanwhile, the prospects are not good for increasing or even maintaining the flows of aid and official finance to the region. Politically, the needs of Eastern Europe and the former Soviet Union are far more pressing than Latin America's. Despite official denials, a large proportion of the third world's traditional allocations of aid and credit are likely to be diverted to the ex-Communist countries.

Of course, there are positive developments on the horizon. The North American Free Trade Area (NAFTA) could lock Mexico firmly into the U.S. economy and its democratic political structures. Gradually, the same mechanism could be extended to Central America and even the Western Hemisphere as a whole. In recent years, the private capital markets have been rediscovering Latin America, and the swelling of direct investment, along with the return of flight capital, could more than make up for the declines in official financing. In terms of know-how and entrepreneurial vigor, direct investment will contribute much more to the Latin economies than would the corresponding amount of bank lending or intergovernmental flows of funds.

On balance, however, external conditions in the 1990s are likely to be as difficult for Latin America as they were in the last decade. How then can Latin American countries break out of their economic stagnation, offer more hope to their people, and help to consolidate the democratic achievements of the past decade?

The answer from the United States and the industrialized world is unanimous and simple: by their own efforts. This message may be harsh, but Latin Americans must understand it. In the post-Communist world order, political attention will be focused elsewhere, and, with the possible exception of Mexico, Latin American countries can expect no special consideration from the industrialized countries, even the United States. But the world's relative lack of interest need not imply that Latin America must survive in the 1990s without financial inflows or that it must simply grin and bear it when confronting protectionist trade barriers in the industrialized world. On the contrary, the new post-Communist world order will require Latin American countries to play a much more active role in international economic diplomacy. They will have to attend to their own interests instead of waiting for leadership from Washington.

For example, those countries that have not already negotiated substantial debt forgiveness will have to show more initiative in relieving themselves of their remaining burdens. Debt relief will become even more important than it was in the 1980s as the flow of official finance continues to dry up. In fact, in the decade ahead, the formal cancellation of debts is likely to be the most reliable source of development financing available to the region. The only other major source of new foreign exchange will be equally unconventional—reductions in military purchases from the United States and Europe.

Beyond that, Latin American and other developing countries will have to exert pressure to make the industrialized world live up to its rhetoric about free trade and free capital movement. If the export-oriented development model now being adopted across Latin America turns out to be successful, U.S. industries will tend to move from Ohio and California to take advantage of Latin America's cheap labor, low social overheads, and lax environmental regulations. Washington will be inundated with demands for protection, most of them cloaked in legitimate humanitarian and environmental concerns.

Will politicians in the United States and other industrialized countries stick to their free market principles and resist such protectionist agitation? Will they face up to financial reality and finally require their banks to forgive the bulk of Latin America's debts? Will Latin America's impoverished citizens and restless soldiers have the patience to find out?

As the essays in this book show, questions like these are hanging over the future of every Latin American country. None of them can yet be answered. All that can be said with certainty is that Latin America is in a period of radical transition. Politically, it is a time of hope unprecedented in the region's modern history. Economically, too, these countries seem poised for takeoff. Will the rocket fly skywards, crash in a fireball, or just sputter on the launching pad? The answer will depend on luck, the state of the world economy, and the policies of the United States and other industrialized countries. But above all it will depend on the Latin Americans themselves.

Notes

1. Anatole Kaletsky, *The Costs of Default* (New York: Priority Press Publications, 1985), p. 106. See also *International Debt and the Stability of the World Economy* (Washington, D.C.: Institute for International Economics, 1983) and *International Debt: Systematic Risk and Policy Response* (Washington, D.C.: Institute for International Economics, 1984).

2. Pedro Aspe, "Stabilization & Structural Change: The Mexican Experience," Lionel Robbins Memorial Lectures, MIT Press, forthcoming.

2 / Political and Economic Challenges for Chile's Transition to Democracy

Arturo Valenzuela

The wave of democracy sweeping the world in the final two decades of the twentieth century has led to the election of heads of state in relatively open, fair contests in all countries of Latin America save Cuba. Chile, historically noted for its democratic traditions, was one of the last countries in the hemisphere to return to representative government after a long interlude of authoritarianism. On December 14, 1989, Chileans went to the polls and elected Patricio Aylwin, a respected former Christian Democratic senator, to the presidency. Aylwin's triumph at the head of a broad center-left coalition, which had vehemently opposed the military regime of General Augusto Pinochet, marked a peaceful and promising finale to the country's sixteen years of dictatorship.

The success of the Concertación, as the governing coalition is known, and its parallel victory in congressional races held the same day, represented a stunning political setback for army commander Pinochet, who had presided over the nation since the 1973 overthrow of the elected government of Socialist president Salvador Allende. The general had been personally humiliated a year earlier in a plebiscite designed to ratify his own continuation in office until 1997. In the open presidential contest that followed, Pinochet's former minister of finance, Hernán Büchi, a wunderkind technocrat who had forged the final stage of Chile's bold experiment in free market economics, was defeated by the heterogeneous and often querulous array of opponents whom Pinochet had denounced and disdained for years.

Chile's transition to democracy may prove to be one of the most successful in Latin America. In large measure, this is true because Chile's experience is one of redemocratization rather than of democratic construction. Successful cases of transition to democracy result less from the circumstances that contributed to regime breakdown, the character of the dictatorial regime, or the nature of the transition process itself than from the country's historic experience with democratic governance.

Chile, despite the severe crisis that led to the overthrow of constitutional government in 1973, had previously one of the strongest records of democratic rule in the third world. From 1830 until 1973, with the exception of fourteen months of unconstitutional rule, every president was duly elected to office and made way for his elected successor. That democratic tradition, which included a powerful legislature, a history of fair elections, viable political parties, a strong state, and widespread respect for the rule of law and constitutional procedures, is an invaluable asset in the delicate process of democratic reconsolidation. Neighboring countries such as Argentina, Brazil, Peru, and Bolivia face the daunting task of building party structures and democratic institutions while simultaneously confronting the difficult challenges of economic stability, growth, and popular demands for better living standards.

Although Chile's preexisting institutions and democratic practices are critical to understanding the Chilean transition, the move to democratic rule was aided significantly by economic and political developments unfolding in the authoritarian period and continuing through its demise. By contrast with the experience of newly instituted civilian governments in neighboring countries, which inherited bleak economic conditions from their military predecessors, Chile's new government came to office in March 1990 with one of the most favorable pictures for growth and development in the region. Unlike their counterparts throughout the continent, the Chilean military had succeeded in implementing far-reaching structural reforms that revolutionized the Chilean state and revitalized the economy.

In its first year in power, the new democratic government not only retained but enhanced the confidence of the international financial community and foreign investors. The country's debt maturities were rolled over for the 1991–94 period, and Chile placed a $200 million Eurobond issue with prominent banks. The value of Chilean debt paper increased on the secondary market, trading at 90 percent of face value, the highest rate for any Latin American country.[1] Chile became the first country in the region to sign a bilateral debt reduction agreement with the United States within the framework of the Enterprise for the Americas Initiative. In 1990, foreign investments of $1.1 billion dollars helped the country post a record $2.4 billion balance of payments surplus.[2]

Chile's transition has also been aided by the survival of the country's long-standing political parties of the center and left. Linked by their common rejection of the military government and its legacy, socialists, Christian Democrats, and social democrats were able to set aside their differences and draw on their formidable organizational capacity to overcome the twin challenges of insurrectionary groups seeking the violent overthrow of the military government and the repressive measures of the authorities seeking to perpetuate their own rule. Today these parties (especially the Christian Democratic party, the Socialist party and the Party for Democracy), with strong ties to the nation's ubiquitous secondary associations, such as labor unions, community organizations, student groups, and trade associations, have forged a unified government that, after a year in office, retains a high level of popular support.[3]

And yet, despite the promise of Chile's transition in the early months, it is still too early to judge whether the country will fully recover its democratic traditions and consolidate its governing institutions in a workable fashion in the near future. Over the next months and years, Chileans face difficult challenges that will test severely the country's efforts to build a better future.

Chile's transition is one in which institutions, vested interests, and unresolved conflicts from the past are still very much present. The society remains divided, with well-articulated political tendencies embracing sharply different interpretations of recent history and alternative visions of the future. While the experience of authoritarianism, the crisis in world socialism, and the emerging consensus over the appropriateness of market economies has narrowed the polarization that bedeviled the years leading up to the military coup, Chile contains explosive political forces that could reappear in the future.

The room for maneuver of the new authorities, while substantial, is clearly circumscribed by the continued influence of the rules, procedures, and players of the previous regime. While the remnants of this authoritarian past have facilitated the transition in the short term, they may set back the emerging consensus on the democratic rules of the game and eventually prove destabilizing.

The Economic Sphere

The most dramatic change that took place under military rule was the successful implementation of ambitious economic reforms aimed at curtailing the broad reach of the state into Chile's economic affairs. With the full blessing of the four military commanders and the unique powers afforded by dictatorial rule, a sophisticated team of civilian technocrats and economists—many trained at the University of Chicago—systematically dismantled the model of state-protected import substitution industrialization, which had been implemented after the Great Depression and deepened by the reformist and socialist policies of the Frei and Allende governments between 1964 and 1973. Indeed, even before the advent of the Allende presidency in 1970, the Chilean state had controlled a larger portion of the economy than any other Latin American country except for Cuba.[4]

The "Chicago Boys" were supported in their efforts by the military commanders, in particular General Pinochet. A reluctant convert to free market economics, Pinochet nevertheless admired the scientific certainty of his economic team and their independence from vested interests. They also benefited because Chile's entrepreneurial elite had been politically weakened by the Frei and Allende experiments and were not in a position to combat free market policies, even if many of these were injurious to their own traditional interests. For many firms, the military government had meant salvation from what they had perceived to be certain death. They were not about to criticize their saviors, no matter how painful the economic remedies might be.

The military government's latitude was also enhanced by the simple fact that it inherited an economy in shambles. Inflation was running over 500 percent per year, the country's international reserves had been depleted, and the government deficit had skyrocketed to the equivalent of 25 percent of GDP. State-owned and expropriated firms, employing over 5 percent of the workforce, were losing $500 million a year, a sum equivalent to over a third of the value of the nation's exports.[5]

Over the next seven years, the military's economic team eliminated Chile's chronic fiscal deficit, privatized state enterprises, dismantled tariff barriers (from an average of 90 percent down to 10 percent), created a viable capital market, sharply reduced the power of labor unions, and began a process of shifting state services to the private sector and to local authorities.[6]

By 1976, Chile's economy began to respond to these stimuli, growing over the next five years at an average rate of 8 percent per year, fueled by a dramatic expansion in nontraditional exports. Representing 12 percent of GDP in 1970, exports climbed to 24 percent by 1980. The country's reversal of fortune led members of Chile's economic team to crow that "in ten more years Chile will be a developed country."[7]

This optimism, however, proved much too premature. By 1982, Chile's economy had collapsed, a victim of the downturn in the world economy, rampant speculation, and serious policy errors on the part of Pinochet's economic managers. In particular, the imposition of a fixed-dollar exchange rate, in an attempt to control inflation, had contributed to a severe overvaluation of the Chilean currency, accompanied by sharp increases in spending on imported consumer goods and massive international indebtedness. At the same time, the lack of regulation of the banking sector had encouraged speculative borrowing and large-scale lending to risky enterprises, including many newly privatized state firms owned by the lenders.

As a result, per capita growth rates plunged 16.7 percent in 1982–83, as countless firms failed and the banking system collapsed. The government was forced to take over the private financial system and many of the bankrupt firms, leading to even greater state control of the economy than during the Allende years. By 1984, Chile's international debt of $20.7 billion had exceeded the nation's GDP and represented a per capita debt higher than that of any other country. Interest payments reached 12 percent of GDP, twice the figure for Mexico or Brazil.[8]

Chile's serious economic predicament was aggravated further in that the economic reform process did not immediately generate increases in employment and improvements in living standards. Throughout most of the Pinochet years, Chile had one of the highest levels of urban unemployment on the continent and, during the first decade of military rule, real wages fell 40 percent, returning to 1970 levels only by 1989.[9]

Finally, the initial opening of the Chilean economy did not generate strong domestic investment. Average investment rates in the 1973–1983 period had fallen to 12 percent, by contrast with 17 percent in the previous decade.[10] It is, therefore, not surprising that some analysts judged the Chilean experiment in free market economics to be a failure and the country's debt burden an insurmountable obstacle to full economic recovery within the foreseeable future.[11]

Yet, over the longer term, Chile's policymakers proved their doubters and detractors wrong. Their concerted and careful implementation of a structural adjustment program involving substantial public savings, coupled with high copper prices and strong support from international financial institutions, led to a significant turnaround in the Chilean economy, without the specter of hyperinflation that plagued many of Chile's neighbors. Private sector firms that had fallen into state hands with the collapse of the banking system were reprivatized, although they were generally sold off without their debts, which were assumed by the government through loans from the Central Bank.

From 1985 until 1989 the country's GNP grew at an average of 6.5 percent, while exports surged 10.1 percent, and inflation remained at 20 percent. Together with Colombia, Chile was the only major economy on the continent to finish the decade with a per capita GDP superior to that of 1980 (although per capita consumption was still lower), and it was the only highly indebted country to avoid an inflationary explosion.

In pursuing its objective, Chile's economic team sought to restructure and refinance the foreign debt while instituting innovative debt conversion schemes. By 1989, the foreign debt had fallen to 64 percent of GDP. Because of net inflows of capital from diverse sources, including World Bank structural adjustment loans and debt-for-equity swaps, combined with significant increases in exports, the country's effective debt service during the 1985–89 period was equivalent to an average of only 9 percent of export earnings, as opposed to 24 percent for Latin America as a whole.[12]

While the economic stabilization policies of the eighties proved very effective, it is unlikely that they would have worked had the Chilean structural adjustment process not begun a decade earlier. Chile's economy was able to respond to the more stable and predictable macroeconomic climate of the late 1980s precisely because it had already achieved over a period of time an open economy, a viable capital market, relatively low tax levels, and an increasingly dynamic private sector.

By the time Patricio Aylwin was elected to the presidency, the Chilean economy had evolved from one of the most protected in Latin America to one of the most open. Chile had been transformed from a country of inefficient domestic industries, overly reliant on copper exports, to one of vigorous and diversified exports and streamlined manufacturing operations. The state had been pared down significantly, with most public enterprises privatized and many regulations and subsidies discontinued. As the 1980s came to an end, foreign investors "discovered" Chile and dollars began to flow into the country, contributing further to the economic upsurge.

The success of these changes, and the new government's recognition that they must be maintained and strengthened, makes it unlikely that

Chile will return to the status quo ante, in which a benevolent interventionist state sheltered inefficient industries for much of the twentieth century, even as intense ideological rivalries led to repeated wild swings in other national policies. Indeed, the Aylwin government's economic team has earned high praise for maintaining macroeconomic stability while seeking ways to address some of the social problems that still plague the country. The new authorities face serious challenges in ensuring that Chile's newfound prosperity will benefit more than just a small portion of the population and that the country's continued inequities (close to 40 percent of national households live in poverty) will not bring pressure to shift toward a more populist economic strategy.[13]

The Political Sphere

Chile's transition to democracy was facilitated by the failure of each of the most powerful political actors in the country to achieve its fundamental objectives. They were all, to a greater or lesser extent, "defeated."

Chile's military rulers had rejected the notion that political liberalization should accompany economic liberalization, and sought to perpetuate authoritarian policies with minimal concessions to demands for the restoration of fundamental freedoms. Just as Pinochet and his aides were able to engineer an open economy, they were convinced that they could create a "modern and protected democracy," in which disruptive ideological struggles were replaced by smooth vertical and hierarchical political relationships under military tutelage.

For years after the coup of 1973, Chile remained a nation of enemies, a country divided into silent ghettos, where opponents were persecuted and marginalized, cut off from the mainstream of national life.[14] In this oppressive atmosphere, political opposition remained dormant and ineffectual for a decade. Some groups on the left sought in vain to develop an insurrectionary capacity that would lead to the overthrow of the regime and the imposition of an "advanced democracy."

Others began trying to mend the threads of democratic parties and social movements that had been torn asunder by the ideological polarization of the early 1970s and the crackdown that followed the military coup. Chile's military rulers were convinced, however, that the parties and leaders of the past had already been relegated to the dustbin of history, too divided to cooperate and too out of touch to challenge their authority and economic success. With a new generation of Chileans raised in an atmosphere where economic choice replaced politics,

Pinochet and his colleagues believed the ideological conflicts of the past would become obsolete, and that a new political order, based on the military principles of patriotism, hierarchy, and obedience, would emerge triumphant.

After eight years of strong-arm rule, the government designed a new constitution and orchestrated its adoption in a 1980 referendum without electoral guarantees. The charter gave Pinochet extensive powers to curtail basic rights and provided for no competitive elections until 1997, twenty-four years after the military coup. Instead, it called for a plebiscite in late 1988 or 1989 to ratify as president for an eight-year term the candidate chosen by the four armed forces commanders. It was no secret that Pinochet, the army commander, expected to be chosen to succeed himself, and effectively to occupy the presidency for life —much as his hero, Francisco Franco, had done in Spain.

The authorities' calculations began to unravel with the massive protests that broke out in 1983, following the sharp reversal of Chile's economic fortunes the previous year. To the visible consternation of Pinochet and his aides, the much-vilified labor unions, civic groups, and political parties of the past began to recuperate, gradually knitting a web of organizations determined to challenge the political monopoly of the armed forces.

Under near-impossible conditions, in the face of systematic regime efforts to discredit and destroy them, Chile's democratic parties began a slow process of soul-searching, compromise, and regeneration. By the late 1980s, groups from the socialist left to the moderate right had joined in the democratic coalition against military rule. After a period of intense debate, they reluctantly agreed to play by the rules they despised in order to battle the dictator at the polls. Ironically, the regime welcomed this challenge and agreed to a fair contest, confident that Pinochet would win the plebiscite and prove to the world that he, and not the opposition, had the support of Chile's "silent majorities." With the triumph of the opposition forces in the October 5, 1988, contest, there was nothing the regime could do but accept the results and call for free and open elections within a year as the charter dictated. General Pinochet was beaten at his own game, unable to sustain himself as the leader of the institutional order he had created for himself.

With the defeat of Pinochet and Hernán Büchi in the open presidential race a year later, Chile's rightists found themselves unable to carry out what had seemed a natural succession from the military regime. Leaders of the right had become convinced that the regime's rhetoric was correct, that the politics of ideology and "demagoguery" had been replaced by the politics of a grateful people schooled in the virtues of free market economics. Chile's reinvigorated right, representing the new dynamism of industry and commerce, hoped to project the military government's success into the future, drawing on a new generation of leaders. Instead, racked by internal dissent fueled by personal ambitions and generational conflicts, the right found itself in a distinct minority, and protected from a worse defeat only by an electoral system deliberately designed to benefit its candidates.

On the other side of the political spectrum, Chile's far left, dominated by one of the largest Communist parties in the West, met an even more devastating setback at the hands of a political process it failed to fully understand, in a country unwilling to embark on an insurrectionary course. The Communists and their allies had envisioned a popular uprising reminiscent of the Sandinista insurrection against Somoza in Nicaragua. Under that scenario, they believed they, as the new vanguard of the revolution, would be able to press for the establishment of socialism with the mass support of a populace devastated by the trauma of the military government's economic policies and repressive actions. Central to this plan was an embrace of armed struggle as a critical component of its strategy to challenge the military's dominance of force, which led to hundreds of bombings by urban guerrilla groups and a frustrated assassination attempt against Pinochet in September of 1986.

But the Communist left did not succeed in luring the masses to its vision of violent opposition and apocalyptic change. Instead, the politics of consensus and peaceful opposition gathered force and momentum throughout the 1980s. The years of division, repression, and struggle against authoritarian rule forged a gradual transformation of Chile's political class, eroding its culture of confrontation and conflict and replacing it with one encouraging compromise and consensus. These changes represented not merely a temporary strategy against a common enemy; they were a profound recognition of past errors and of the need to adapt to modern times with a more genuinely democratic style of politics.

Of particular importance was the sea change in the large socialist left, which began to abandon its Marxist-Leninist precepts even before the sweeping decline of European and Soviet Marxism became visible to the world. The results of this transformation are evident in the Aylwin government, where socialists now serve as cabinet ministers, energetically implementing free market economic policies and championing "bourgeois democracy" as an end in itself, and not simply as a means for the achievement of other aims.

Victorious in the 1988 plebiscite and 1989 election, the democratic parties nonetheless failed to achieve their most cherished objective. For years they had sought not only the defeat of General Pinochet, but the complete rejection of his transition schedule and proposed institutional order. They never accepted the 1980 constitution as valid, arguing that it was fundamentally undemocratic and illegitimate.

Yet, in agreeing to the framework spelled out in that document in order to defeat the general within "his own legality," the democratic opposition effectively granted legitimacy to the institutional arrangements they had so despised. The military regime and the opposition parties did agree to a meaningful set of constitutional reforms, ratified by a referendum prior to the open presidential election in 1989, but they did not substantially change the Pinochet constitution. The opposition also succeeded in reversing the prohibition of parties and leaders seen by the military as ideologically undesirable, reducing the role of the National Security Council as a potential military veto on civilian authorities, and obtaining more flexible provisions for future constitutional reform. However, the agreed-upon reforms also tacitly acknowledged the 1980 constitution as the fundamental law of the land.[15]

As a result, civilian leaders have to deal not only with the physical omnipresence of the military, but also with the many laws, institutions, and policies inherited from the outgoing authoritarian government. The armed forces were given license to run their own affairs, virtually free of civilian supervision. The authoritarian legacy also saddled the country with a highly skewed electoral system, with the continued presence of former regime officials and sympathizers in the legislature and bureaucracy, and with the excessive weight of presidential authority contained in the 1980 constitutional framework.

The most problematic "authoritarian enclave" for Chile's new democratic leaders is the military institution itself. Under statutes that can only be modified by more than a simple majority of both houses of parliament, the armed forces retain full control over their internal affairs, including promotions, education, and procurement policies. Their budgetary allocations are not easily changed and they are guaranteed a fixed percentage of copper sales, Chile's leading export. After Pinochet's electoral defeat, the army transferred numerous state properties to itself. It also incorporated into its ranks the remnants of the former secret police, making clear it would vehemently oppose any effort to prosecute armed forces personnel for the widespread human rights abuses of the 1970s.

A particularly vexing legacy of the past is Pinochet himself. The 1980 constitution allows him to remain commander in chief of the army until 1997, when he will be eighty-two years old. Even though President Aylwin, upon taking office, asked "his" commander to resign, Pinochet declined to step out of the limelight, arguing that he needs to ensure that "not one of my men will be touched." In a curious parallel with the situation in Nicaragua, the newly elected leaders have had to live with the tense reality of continued military privilege and control. The same individual who ruled the country with an iron hand for sixteen years remains the commander of the nation's most powerful military force.

In his first year in office, President Aylwin did not shy away from impressing his superior civilian authority on Pinochet, and he succeeded in gaining the support of the other service commanders, over Pinochet's objections, in asserting presidential prerogatives in the National Security Council. The president also admonished Pinochet repeatedly for speaking about matters outside his realm of competence and gained a tangible victory when his refusal to support the promotion of two top generals was ratified as proper by the comptroller general. In addition, he sought to establish closer working ties with the air force and police as countervailing forces to the army.

The most difficult issue in civil-military relations has been human rights. While the governing coalition had committed itself to establishing the truth of official repression and bringing those responsible for human rights violations to justice, its room for maneuver has been severely circumscribed. The Pinochet regime adopted an amnesty law in 1978, which the courts interpreted as barring any trials, let alone convictions, of armed forces personnel for repressive activities.

The adamant opposition by the military, and the unwillingness of the parties of the right to criticize the armed forces, meant that the new government was stymied in its objective of prosecuting the most serious human rights violations. Although Aylwin was widely praised for appointing a blue-ribbon panel that officially confirmed a systematic pattern of military human rights abuses and promised to press the courts to consider serious cases not covered by the amnesty law, the military and its supporters have effectively frustrated the search for justice for the nearly one thousand people who disappeared without a trace and countless others who suffered torture, arrest, and exile.

Although Pinochet and the army's image has been damaged by various financial scandals and by continued revelations of human rights abuses in the first few months of the civilian government, Chile's military establishment remains very powerful, suspicious of the politicians, and a latent threat to democratic government. Military leaders are convinced that their government was the most successful in the nation's history and confident that they can still govern far better than their civilian counterparts should the need arise again.

Adding to the new government's difficulties are constitutional provisions and legislation enacted by the former junta that prevented the governing coalition, despite Aylwin's landslide in the voting, from winning control of the Congress. Through gerrymandering, the application of an unusual electoral law favoring the minority over the majority, and the appointment of one-fourth of the Senate by Pinochet, the junta managed to give its partisans substantial representation in the House and a two-seat controlling majority in the Senate. This meant that the far-reaching constitutional changes envisioned by the new government would prove unattainable, and that the authorities would have to negotiate every piece of legislation and every constitutional amendment with their former adversaries.

During the first year of democratic government, compromises on several important issues were reached with the moderate rightist Renovación Nacional (RN) party, leading to legislative progress. In particular, RN showed a willingness to work with the government to enact a law increasing taxes to pay for social welfare expenditures and a law modifying some of the provisions of the junta's labor legislation. Constitutional agreements were reached to reform the military justice system, free prisoners who had been charged with political crimes by the military authorities, and, after much debate, permit popular election of local authorities, opening the way for municipal elections in the second quarter of 1992. By the end of 1991, however, rightist parties, after observing a steady decline of support in the polls, signaled their intention to oppose the government more vehemently and to be less forthcoming on legislative and constitutional issues.

The new government also found itself presiding over a complex bureaucracy, which had been molded for sixteen years by Pinochet and his aides. Civil service laws prevented the firing of state employees and severely restricted new appointments. On taking office, President Aylwin found that 320 of 355 mayors, all appointed by his predecessor, could not be removed from office. The Supreme Court, largely filled by

Pinochet appointees after the junta offered lucrative retirement incentives to its older members, has been deeply suspicious of the new government and defensive about charges that it was an accomplice of the military regime in the violation of human rights. Other state employees in the diplomatic corps, the Constitutional Tribunal, the comptroller general's office, and other key agencies owe their careers to Pinochet and have been hostile to the objectives and leadership of President Aylwin and his ministers.

The Pinochet constitution envisioned a powerful executive dominating a weak legislature, which was banished by the outgoing government to the port city of Valparaiso. The president has extensive powers to initiate and mold legislation and to enact many rules through executive decrees. The Congress also lost many of the oversight functions that it had enjoyed in the past when it stood as one of the most powerful legislatures in the hemisphere. Ironically, the Aylwin government has made ample use of these prerogatives, engineering most agreements on major pieces of legislation with party leaders outside of the legislative arena. This has increased tension between the executive branch and the legislature. The public perceives that many decisions are hammered out by a few top leaders without much participation by other elected officials, let alone party activists and rank and file citizens.

Although these authoritarian legacies have frustrated Chile's new authorities, there is no doubt that Chile's transition has been aided in the short term by the "veto power" that the military and the right continue to enjoy. Had the Concertación pressed for an immediate modification of Pinochet's institutional edifice and attempted to dismiss many of his supporters, the armed forces would have been far more resistant to the return of civilian rule. Chile's rightist parties, which remain suspicious of popular sovereignty and fearful that a center-left alliance with majority support could threaten their survival, would have been much more likely to conspire with the military had their guarantees been undermined. These authoritarian legacies have also contributed to the success of the transition by helping the broad coalition under Aylwin's leadership to achieve unity, retain it, and elaborate a common program of moderate policies. This moderation can be attributed not only to respect for a new style of politics after the traumatic years of authoritarian rule, but also to the authorities' genuine fear of the strength of the armed forces and its rightist supporters.

The electoral law, designed to give the right a majority in Congress by encouraging the division of the democratic opposition, had the opposite effect of uniting the sixteen parties opposed to the military government. The opposition agreed to a common list of candidates on the basis of a rough perception of relative party strength, burying historic rivalries and animosities in favor of a single grand coalition. The slim rightist Senate majority of two seats, guaranteed by the presence of nine "designated senators," further encouraged discipline among parties of the governing coalition when they sought to extract concessions from the right on critical legislative matters.

At the same time, the legislative veto power of the right and the implicit threat from an autonomous army have given the Concertación more authority to call on its allies in the labor movement and its supporters among the dispossessed to exercise restraint in their demands for better living standards and redress for the past regime's human rights abuses. The crisis in the Communist party, which split badly after the success of the democratic opposition and the crisis of world socialism, meant that the government did not have to face a parallel challenge from the Marxist left. This has permitted the authorities to pursue conservative fiscal and economic policies aimed at maintaining macroeconomic stability and to avoid antagonizing the armed forces over the thorny issue of human rights violations.

Finally, Pinochet's presence as army commander has been a daily and tangible reminder of the need to retain consensus and unity. The general's departure might improve the prospects for normalizing civil-military relations and rejuvenating the officer corps, but it would have the unintended effect of encouraging greater divisiveness in the potentially fractious coalition governing the country in these delicate transitional months. In the short run, Pinochet may prove to be a greater asset to the Concertación in active service than he would be in retirement. Over the long run, however, his continued presence only postpones the achievement of civilian authority over the military.

The Challenges of the Future

Chile's transition has proceeded smoothly as the country's economic managers have skillfully maintained macroeconomic stability, continued to attract foreign investments, and encouraged export promotion. At the same time, the politicians have lowered their tone and abandoned demands for all-encompassing solutions, instead seeking avenues for bargaining and accommodation. The economic, institutional, and political legacy of the military government and the national trauma that it reflected has forced Chileans on both sides of the political divide to be more realistic, to begin to value compromise, and to accept outcomes that fall short of preferred objectives.

On the economic front, the first year of the democratic government was one of adjustment. The military government's election-year expansionary fiscal and monetary policy led to an unsustainable 10 percent growth rate in 1989, which, along with increases in the value-added tax and petroleum prices during the Gulf war, caused consumer prices to rise by 27.2 percent in 1990. GDP growth in 1990 dropped to 2.2 percent as a result of adjustment-induced contraction in demand, particularly for manufactured products, and exports experienced their lowest growth rate since 1985.

While the economy recovered in early 1991 and growth rates are projected to be around 5 percent for the year, the country continues to face serious inflationary strains. Improvements in real wages and increases in social spending will help the government meet some of its social goals, but at the risk of increasing inflation. Inflationary pressures also stem from the Central Bank's long-term financing requirements for obligations incurred by the military government during the banking collapse of 1982–83. By 1991, these accounted for a staggering 43 percent of the Central Bank assets and represent a net drain on the Central Bank's resources. Chile's inflationary problems are also complicated by the significant inflow of capital into the Chilean economy from foreign investors wanting to capitalize on the country's sound economic reputation.

Over the long run, Chile's economic managers face several difficult challenges. There is broad consensus that the country's economic future depends on a dynamic export sector. While substantial investments in minerals and forestry promise future growth in those areas, the markets for Chile's fruit and fisheries industries have become progressively saturated. This trend, combined with declines in local petroleum and gas production, means that Chile must aggressively pursue new market strategies for export promotion.

While foreign investors will continue to be interested in Chile, it is doubtful whether current investment levels can be maintained, particularly as other economies in the region begin to stabilize and grow. This means that the country will have to increase domestic savings in order to generate the investment needed for future economic growth. Historically, private sector investment has been very weak in Chile. Its expansion in the 1985–89 period was due primarily to public savings resulting from tight fiscal policies and the bonanza in copper prices. Public savings increased from 0.6 percent in 1984 to 9.9 percent in 1989. Over the next few years, the state will have to encourage private investment by maintaining macroeconomic stability, improving further the system of taxation, aggressively identifying new export ventures for private development, and continuing to develop long-term capital markets.[16]

Such a policy, however, will inevitably conflict with pressure from society to increase consumption. The Concertación defeated General Pinochet with the slogan "Happiness is coming" and defeated Hernán Büchi with the slogan "The people win." And yet, because the government was forced to implement a sharp economic adjustment policy during its first year in office, household spending in 1990 dropped in relation to 1989. As President Aylwin comes to the midpoint of his presidency, expressions of discontent over bread-and-butter issues have been growing among ordinary Chileans, who have waited patiently for tangible improvements in their standard of living. Brief strikes in the copper and coal industry, as well as illegal strikes by government employees in the health and education sectors, are indications of an emerging militancy among rank and file workers increasingly disposed to taking matters into their own hands in pressing for higher wages. Other issues, such as a dramatic increase in delinquency and continuing terrorist attacks, including the April 1991 assassination of Chile's most prominent conservative senator, Jaime Guzmán Errázuriz, have added to the climate of uncertainty, even though President Aylwin himself retains high levels of support.

At the same time, the very style of the Concertación, with its quest for consensus and broad agreements among an elite group, has contributed to disenchantment among many midlevel leaders and party members who increasingly object to the lack of genuine channels for participation. Recent polling data reveals an increase in the number of citizens who describe themselves as independent, and a decline in support for all parties and leaders.[17]

Over the long run, Chile's ability to promote further growth, economic well-being, and social peace will depend on the political system's capacity to respond to socioeconomic demands and concerns while maintaining public trust and economic stability. The Aylwin government's success thus far can be attributed to the outstanding leadership of the Ministry of Finance, the strong determination of the Concertación to maintain unity of purpose in the pursuit of common objectives, and the continued willingness of the average citizen to give the new government a chance to prove itself. Indeed, no Chilean government this century has enjoyed as solid a coalition behind it and as much support from the population at large.

It is legitimate to ask, however, whether the "politics of forced compromises," as the speaker of the Chamber of Deputies has called the Chilean transition, will successfully evolve into enduring coalitions with broad popular support, capable of addressing the country's needs, or whether those coalitions will disintegrate, engendering political confrontation reminiscent of Chilean politics in the preauthoritarian period. The nation has yet to return to normal elections and genuine political competition. Because of the peculiarities of Pinochet's electoral law, all parties, including those on the right that supported the military, felt compelled in 1990 to enter into artificial pacts in order to maximize their electoral fortunes. For the sixteen parties of the opposition, the Concertación proved essential to defeat Pinochet and win a majority of the seats in the legislature, but it also meant that each party had to put aside its own electoral aspirations while a handful of party leaders agreed on how many candidates each party would be allotted and in what jurisdictions.[18]

As Chile returns to political "normalcy," the imperatives of that electoral alliance have begun to dissipate, and each party appears anxious to prove that it can command significant popular support. Aylwin's Christian Democrats are convinced that legislators from small center parties, as well as the larger socialists, were elected to Congress on Christian Democratic coattails. Many Christian Democrats are anxious to flex their own muscle in municipal elections scheduled for 1992 and are less disposed to be "generous" to their coalition partners as the 1993 presidential race approaches.

Socialist leaders, on the other hand, while conceding that they may have gained seats from the joint list with the Christian Democrats, now believe that their party and the new Party for Democracy founded by socialists have gained broad support and deserve to run their own slate of candidates. Ricardo Lagos, Aylwin's minister of education and leader of the Socialist group, is one of the two or three most popular figures in Chile, giving strength to the argument that the socialists should run on a separate list headed by Lagos.

Influential leaders in both the Socialist and Christian Democratic ranks warn against the potential breakup of the Concertación. They argue that the alliance could easily win the next eight-year presidential term if it stays together and buries its differences. They also warn that running separate lists could drive a strong wedge into the coalition, contributing at best to policy incoherence and at worst to a significant falling out among the Concertación parties and leaders. Open competition could fan the temptation for populist appeals and make it increasingly difficult to maintain the disciplined economic and social policies required for long-term economic success. The volatility of the electoral law, where a shift of a relatively small percentage of the vote could lead to a significant drop in congressional representation, adds to the feeling of uncertainty and the potential for serious misunderstandings among political elites.[19]

It appears, however, that this argument is losing ground among leaders of the Concertación and that political tensions are rising. There are few Christian Democrats willing to support a socialist as the presidential candidate of the coalition in the next presidential race for fear that such a strategy would damage the party's own electoral appeal and front-runner status at a time of considerable doctrinal confusion. Their assumption is that the presidential candidate should once again come from their ranks in exchange for some concessions in legislative races.

Socialists and leaders of the Party for Democracy, on the other hand, wonder whether playing second fiddle to the Christian Democrats over the next decade might not irreparably damage their chances to establish themselves as a viable center-left option for the future, one capable of also preempting any possible resurgence of a renewed Communist left.

Adding to the temptation to "go it alone" is the provision in the Chilean constitution calling for a second round in the presidential race between the two front-runners, should no candidate obtain an absolute majority. This would allow parties to run their own slates on the first round with the intention of structuring a coalition on the second. Such a strategy, however, is fraught with uncertainty and could increase the temptation to engage in populist appeals in order to maximize voting support in the second round.

The second round is likely to encourage a division on the right as well, between the more moderate Renovación Nacional and the more hard-line Unión Democrática Independiente (UDI), the party closest to the military legacy, both claiming to be the most appropriate heir to the military government. If one adds the likelihood of a candidacy by Francisco Javier Errázuriz, the populist businessman who came close to obtaining as many votes as Büchi did in the 1989 race, it is possible that Chileans will see at least five presidential candidates in the first round of the presidential contest.

With a contentious presidential race scheduled hard on the heels of the mid-1992 municipal election, Chile will find itself in a climate of continuous electoral competition after only two years of democratic rule. Chilean political leaders will have to exercise considerable restraint if they are to build on the lessons of the past and the example of the first transition government to deepen the new spirit of political accommodation and compromise, and thus retain public confidence.

From the evidence so far, including the capacity of leaders in the government and the opposition to come to substantial agreements on important issues, there are grounds for cautious optimism that Chile will be able to ride out the centrifugal forces of the coming electoral contests. Even if the municipal and national races are fought on separate party lists, it is likely that the Concertación will manage to structure the necessary political understanding to build a governing coalition aimed at continuing the work begun by the Aylwin administration. Survey data suggests it is unlikely that the right will be able to win a presidential race in the near future, and indeed could lose support in the legislature, paving the way for a stronger Concertación.

While the approaching electoral contests will be important tests of the maturity of Chile's transition, the failure to enact fundamental constitutional reforms during the Aylwin government is likely to present more significant challenges over the long term. The principal institutional legacy of the Pinochet years, aside from the virtual autonomy of the armed forces, is the exaggerated presidentialism of the system. During the first few months of the Aylwin government, the sharp disparity of authority between the executive branch and the legislature did not lead to overt conflict because of the solidity of the Concertación coalition and the willingness of congressional leaders to defer to executive and party authority to ensure the success of the new government in the face of hostile opponents. Senators and deputies, however, have chafed at their meager role in the legislative process. This style of authority, which was natural to authoritarian Chile, has become increasingly difficult to justify in democratic Chile. With growing partisan disagreements, the gap between presidential and legislative authority has engendered increased animosity between the two governmental branches.

A hostile legislature, with few powers except the negative one of rejecting legislation, can become an obstacle to stable government by tempting the executive branch to govern by decree, thereby aggravating the tensions between the two constitutional powers. The combination of a strong executive and a competitive multiparty system that deprives the executive of majority support in the legislature is a clear formula for governmental instability. Despite the efforts of the military regime, Chilean party politics remains heterogenous, with no single group or tendency capable of commanding majority support in Congress. While two-thirds of all Chileans express party identification, the Christian Democrats as Chile's largest party have fewer than 30 percent of those supporters.[20] Chilean democracy was severely strained in the past by the extraordinary difficulties presidents had in structuring coalitions in the legislature when their parties or coalitions had minority support.

Leaders of the Concertación were well aware of the potential dangers of lopsided executive authority in their far-reaching critique of the Pinochet constitution during their campaign for power. And yet, in office they have been reluctant to raise the issue for fear that it would engender strong opposition in the military and on the right. The government has been overly cautious in dealing with questions of constitutional reform, judging that such issues should not be raised until the final year of Aylwin's term. Renovación Nacional initially noted its willingness to consider constitutional reforms dealing with the balance between governmental powers, and the military proved to be less of a challenge than the authorities feared on issues not directly related to military prerogatives. But as the Aylwin administration moves to its midterm, political leaders have become preoccupied with more immediate concerns and electoral issues and have lost sight of the fundamental changes in the 1980 constitution that they had so vigorously championed before coming to power.

This means that the next democratic government will have to continue to cope with the institutional structure inherited from the authoritarian period, one designed more for strong-man rule and subservient parties than for more democratic government in a strong multiparty context. With time and a continued disposition to work together for the good of the country, Chile's civilian leaders should have the will to enact further reforms aimed at bringing their country fully back into the concert of the world's democracies. If they do not, many of the pressures and conflicts that once brought Chilean democracy to its worst crisis in history could again challenge the nation's long-term political stability.

Notes

1. *Latin American Weekly Report* (August 29, 1991), p. 29.

2. Statistics for this article come from mimeographed circulars. An insightful update on the Chilean economy is in Embassy of the United States, *Chile: Economic Trends* (Santiago: Banco Central de Chile, June 1991).

3. A full description of the Pinochet years in Chile, including an account of the transition process, can be found in Pamela Constable and Arturo Valenzuela, *A Nation of Enemies: Chile Under Pinochet* (New York: W.W. Norton and Co., 1991).

4. Arturo Valenzuela, *The Breakdown of Democratic Regimes: Chile* (Baltimore: Johns Hopkins University Press, 1978), p. 13.

5. Daniel Wisecarver, "Regulación y derregulación en Chile: Septiembre 1973 a Septiembre 1983," *Estudios Públicos* no. 22 (Santiago, Autumn 1986), p. 120.

6. The literature on the Chilean economy is now extensive. See Joseph Ramos, *Neoconservative Economics in the Southern Cone of Latin America: 1973–1983* (Baltimore: Johns Hopkins University Press, 1984); Sebastián Edwards and Alejandra Cox Edwards, *Monetarism and Liberalization: The Chilean Experiment* (Cambridge, Mass.: Ballinger, 1987); and Alvaro Bardón et. al., *Una década de cambios económicos* (Santiago: Andrés Bello, 1985) for a sampling. For a fuller elaboration of the points presented here, see Constable and Valenzuela, *A Nation of Enemies*, Chapters 7, 8, 9.

7. José Piñera, *El Mercurio* (Santiago), August 28, 1980, p. 1.

8. See Rudiger Dornbusch's background paper in *The Road to Economic Recovery: Report of the Twentieth Century Fund Task Force on International Debt* (New York: Priority Press Publications, 1989), p. 61.

9. Pamela Constable and Arturo Valenzuela, "Democracy Restored," *Journal of Democracy* vol. 1, no. 2 (Spring 1990), p. 6.

10. Ramos, *Neoconservative Economics*, p. 48.

11. Dornbusch remarked that "Chile is certainly one of the debtor countries least likely to become solvent." See his *The Road to Economic Recovery*, p. 61.

12. Juan Andrés Fontaine, "Observaciones sobre la experiencia macroeconómica chilena de 1985–1989," *Estudios Públicos (Santiago)*, no. 40 (Spring 1990), p. 205.

13. United Nations, Economic Commission for Latin America and the Caribbean, *Statistical Yearbook for Latin America and the Caribbean* (New York, 1991), p. 45.

14. The following observations are drawn from Constable and Valenzuela, *A Nation of Enemies.*

15. The fact that the reforms agreed to in 1989 did not significantly alter the military's constitution means that the Chilean transition is neither a transition through "pacted reform," where the outgoing regime admits fundamental change in the institutional order, or one of "pacted rupture," where the outgoing regime's order is replaced by a new constitutional formula entirely devised by civilian leaders after a clear break with the past. Spain is an example of the first form, and Greece or Argentina of the second. The Chilean transition is more fully enmeshed in the constitutional legacy of the military government. For these distinctions see Juan J. Linz, "Transitions to Democracy," *Washington Quarterly* (Summer 1990), pp. 143–64.

16. The importance of savings is stressed by Fontaine. Figures are from his "Observaciones sobre la experiencia macroeconómica chilena," p. 212.

17. See "Estudio social y de opinión pública," working paper no. 161, Centro de Estudios Públicos, Santiago, September 1991.

18. For a full discussion of Chile's electoral law and its potential problems, see Arturo Valenzuela and Peter Siavelis, "Ley electoral y estabilidad democrática: Un ejercicio de simulación para el caso de Chile," *Estudios Públicos*, no. 43 (Spring 1991), pp. 27–87.

19. For this argument see Valenzuela and Siavelis, "Ley electoral y estabilidad democrática."

20. See "Estudio social y de opinión pública."

CHILE: ECONOMIC STATISTICS

	1986	1987	1988	1989	1990	1991e
Domestic Economy						
Real GDP (1977 pesos, billions)	376.6	398.2	427.5	470.2	480.3	508.2
% change	5.7	5.7	7.4	10.0	2.1	5.8
Per capita GDP (US$)	1,364	1,511	1,732	1,948	2,110	2,415
Per capita real GDP (% change)	3.9	4.0	5.6	8.2	0.5	4.2
Inflation (% change)	19.5	19.9	14.7	17.0	26.0	21.8
Population (millions)	12.33	12.54	12.75	12.96	13.17	13.38
Unemployment (% of labor force)	8.8	7.9	8.3	6.3	6.0	6.5
Public sector borrowing (% of GDP)	1.9	0.4	-3.6	-2.3	-1.1	-1.0
External Economy (US$ millions)						
Exchange rate (pesos-US$)	193.0	219.5	245.1	267.2	305.1	349.6
Merchandise exports	4,199	5,224	7,052	8,080	8,310	8,929
Merchandise imports	-3,099	-3,994	-4,833	-6,502	-7,037	-7,377
Trade balance	1,100	1,230	2,219	1,578	1,273	1,552
Current account balance	-1,137	-808	-167	-767	-824	93
Total external debt	20,829	20,660	18,960	17,520	18,576	17,224
% of GDP	123.9	109.0	85.9	69.4	66.8	57.3
% of exports goods, services & income	389.4	318.2	224.4	177.8	176.2	154.3
Total debt service	2,572	2,302	2,471	2,704	2,868	2,627
% of exports, goods, services & income	48.1	35.5	29.2	27.4	27.2	23.5

e estimate
Source: The Institute of International Finance

3 / Solving the Peruvian Puzzle

Felipe Ortiz de Zevallos M.

Peru stands at its own peculiar crossroads. It has been more sorely afflicted than any other South American country by populist state interventionism and is severely threatened by terrorist subversion and drug traffickers. The indications of Peru's decline are overwhelming. Just a quick look suggests the possibility of a military coup, impending civil war, or a Pol Pot kind of Maoist insurgency. The state is bankrupt, and whole regions of the country are beset by poverty and social conflict. It is not a situation that the world can long ignore because whatever happens in Peru—for centuries the center of South America—in the next few years will be profoundly felt throughout the continent.

Peru only recently took its first steps away from the edge, under the presidency of a university professor of Japanese descent with no affiliation to any traditional political party. Contrary to all expectations and to his own vague statements during his electoral campaign, a few days after his inauguration, President Alberto Fujimori began a drastic stabilization program in a last-ditch attempt to set fiscal accounts in order, liberalize markets, stop hyperinflation, and restore ties to international lenders. During his first twenty months in office, Fujimori has shown a rare combination of prudence and firmness in dealing with the economic crisis.[1]

The problems Fujimori faces began decades ago. In 1961, the Peruvian economy looked like one of the soundest in Latin America: open, vigorous, and fairly free of state intervention. GDP grew by

7 percent with only 9 percent annual inflation.[2] A discerning analyst, however, would have seen some problems. Peruvian society was still steeped in colonial values, especially in an agricultural sector that was still based upon the primitive hacienda system. Income differences were extreme. The social gap between the white minority and the majority of Andean natives and mestizos made attempts at national integration difficult. Modernization was proceeding very slowly, and there was little grasp of how wealth was created.

Many of these characteristics remained much the same for most of the next thirty years. Meanwhile, almost everything else changed drastically. The open, stable, and growing economy of the early 1960s was gradually strangled by inappropriate state intervention following a leftist military coup in 1968. Prices were controlled, consumer goods subsidized, and private companies expropriated under the guise of improving income distribution, but with gross disregard for fundamental macroeconomic rules. Wealthy Peruvians are far less wealthy today than three decades ago, and the poor are as poor as ever. Per capita income is the same as it was thirty years ago. GDP in 1990 was 10 percent lower than in 1980. Inflation between 1985 and 1990 exceeded 2,000,000 percent. By the end of President Alan García's administration in July 1990, Peru's foreign debt amounted to $22 billion, with $14 billion of this in arrears.[3]

Fujimori has changed the situation dramatically. According to estimates for 1992, annual inflation could fall to less than 50 percent, down from 1991's 140 percent (which was already vastly lower than the four-digit nightmare of the previous administration). GDP growth could surpass 3 percent. However, once this economic emergency is surmounted, a wide range of severe problems await solution: the terrorist subversion; the fight against drug trafficking; the reconstitution of the social contract between the state and the people; and the recovery of a sense of national integration that would give Peru's poorest some hope for the future.

A new society is emerging in response to the crisis. Peru is well endowed by nature and has a rich and ancient culture and a resourceful people. In shantytowns, mothers have formed clubs to keep hunger at bay through communal cooking; doctors earning less than $100 a month have saved hundreds of thousands of lives threatened by cholera; peasants have formed their own armed groups ("rondas") to protect themselves against fanatical guerrillas; artists and scientists persist in their creative endeavors though lacking almost every means of support; a number of self-made entrepreneurs are ready to compete in sophisticated international markets.

Peru could sink even further into the vortex of social and political violence, or it could become a showcase for the rest of Latin America, proof that pragmatism and prudence should prevail over misguided ideologies and demagogic practices. Throughout this transformation, the attitude of the U.S. government is of special importance. Peru needs official financial support for a rational debt restructuring that could provide the basis for productive private investment. The United States and Peru also need a joint strategy to combat drug trafficking, but in a way that does not turn coca-growing peasants into tactical allies of the Shining Path (Sendero Luminoso) guerrillas. In fact, all efforts to help Peru must be evaluated without losing sight of the reality that the government is fighting a serious grass-roots terrorist insurgency.

The Past Two Decades

Throughout the 1970s, Peru was governed by a populist and nationalist left-wing military government that expropriated many foreign and domestic private companies, including all media, implemented an ill-conceived agrarian reform, created an unwieldy state apparatus, and developed state-run heavy industry without heed to whether such investments made sense economically. The international banking community, amazingly, generously backed these ventures, financing many a grandiose project.

Most of the military government's economic measures distorted key markets. Development strategy was almost entirely inward-looking and heavily protectionist. Most imports were subject to prohibitions, quotas, or discretionary tariffs, and there were costly foreign exchange requirements imposed on trade. The financial sector was heavily regulated and burdened with direct government involvement. As a result of the agrarian reform, sale of land and its use as collateral for borrowing were severely restricted. The government forbade private companies to fire workers and required that a percentage of annual profits be distributed freely among them as capital stock, impairing the firms' international competitiveness. As a result, many companies were forced to do business in a "gray market," an informal economy where growth was limited by the lack of legal recognition and clear rules for business.

The military government's policies failed. The economy grew only 3.5 percent a year, against annual increases averaging 5 percent in the

1960s and 6 percent in the 1950s. Inflation rose to more than 70 percent a year. In 1979, under internal social and international pressure, the armed forces agreed to free elections to put civilians back in power.

The 1980 general elections were won by Fernando Belaunde Terry, the same man the military had deposed twelve years earlier. He inherited a stagnant economy. A third of the labor force in the formal non-agricultural sector was made up of public employees. Notoriously inefficient state-owned enterprises—few in 1968—numbered 180 by 1980 and dominated almost every economic sector. The military-imposed legal structure severely discouraged private investment.

Election day in 1980 was also the day chosen by the Shining Path to launch its violent campaign to overthrow the state. This terrorist group was headed by Abimael Guzmán (known also as Presidente Gonzalo), a former university professor in the Andean city of Ayacucho. The rebels had spent the previous decade in underground political work, recruiting cadres and training militants in Peru's isolated southern-central sierra. Interpreting a complex society through the reality of its backward and forgotten elements alone, the Shining Path established itself as the most radical and violent political organization in the Americas. The rebels called for revolution to bring about a peasant-controlled republic, based on Maoist principles, that would be marked by "a new society, without exploited or exploiters, without oppressed or oppressors, without classes, or State, or parties, or democracy, or arms, or war."[4]

Unfortunately, the new government's efforts to correct the structural deficiencies of the economy were halfhearted. Belaunde was less interested in laying the basis for a well-functioning market economy and democratic society than in promoting huge public works in housing and roads. To finance these works, the government borrowed extensively between 1980 and 1982. Indeed, Peru's fiscal deficit and total foreign debt grew considerably faster in this period than those of other Latin American countries. The World Bank timidly supported Peru's ambitions and increased its loans to the country throughout this period.

A series of natural disasters along the Peruvian coast in 1983 compounded the adverse effects of low prices for some basic export commodities. That year, Peru's GDP plummeted 12 percent, the government lost one-seventh of its tax revenues, private debt soared dangerously, and annual inflation hit three digits.

Rising economic distress recruited new players to political violence. In June 1984, the Túpac Amaru Revolutionary Movement (MRTA) launched its own armed actions, including guerrilla warfare in San Martín Department, a region of dense rain forest on the eastern slopes of the Andes. MRTA, a more typical Latin American insurgent group than the Shining Path, asserted that the political system, including the military government, had failed to meet the most urgent needs of Peruvians.

During the final year of the Belaunde government, its last economic team attempted to restore a minimum balance to the economy. The budgetary crisis, however, forced it to default partially on its foreign debt in order to meet domestic needs, with the government remitting payments only when the everyday cash flow permitted.

Peruvians regained much hope when they elected Alan García to the presidency in 1985. Endowed with a popular charisma comparable in Latin American history only to Perón's in Argentina or Castro's in Cuba, he used his power as poorly as they. His administration diagnosed the economy as being in a "debt trap," claiming that servicing the foreign debt was accelerating exchange rate devaluation and inflation and that investment was being curtailed as net transfers of capital abroad eroded domestic savings.

García's government reactivated the economy by boosting consumer demand in order to use idle manufacturing capacity. Real wages were increased while taxes and tariffs for public companies providing energy, water, and other services were reduced in real terms, with negative fiscal results. In an attempt to curtail capital flight and develop domestic industry, the economy was closed off from the rest of the world through a combination of import quotas and controlled exchange rates. Payments on the foreign debt were unilaterally restricted in an unsuccessful attempt to limit them to 10 percent of export revenue.

The economy grew 17 percent during García's first two years in office, but this risky course was unsustainable. The public deficit ballooned out of control, and the current account balance deteriorated severely. There seemed to be no effective way to restore the economy to equilibrium. Public investment was cut to the bone, prices shot out of sight, and corruption flourished throughout the political system. By 1989, production had dropped by 20 percent and real wages had sunk to half their 1985 level, as hyperinflation raged.

Peru's economy was on the verge of total collapse when Alan García left office in July 1990. Tax revenues that month had fallen to 5 percent of GDP. Official prices for controlled goods and public services bore no relation to the costs of producing them. The domestic borrowing requirement of the public sector was nearly 10 percent of GDP, roughly three times the money supply (M2) in domestic currency. July's monthly inflation rate was equivalent to an annual figure of 35,000 percent.

By the end of García's tenure, Peru was suffering from at least two decades of economic mismanagement that was perhaps worse than in any other Latin American country.[5] The raw figures are astounding. By 1990, the capacity to generate electricity was 40 percent below peak levels, while petroleum output was down 60 percent. Road, rail, air, and river transportation systems were all disintegrating, as was the communications network. In 1990 real exports were 40 percent lower than in 1980. Less than 30 percent of Peru's labor force was fully employed with wages above the legal minimum. Public social expenditures—$40 per capita in the early 1980s—had fallen by a third.

At present, half of the Peruvian population lives below the poverty line, with per capita income under $400 a year. Peru's infant mortality rate of 86 per thousand is the third-highest in Latin America. Domestic investment, following the bankruptcy of the public sector, is at an all-time low. Any attempt to maintain basic infrastructure has been abandoned. Liquidity in the formal (above-ground) financial system is half the 1985 level. President García's government exhausted all available international reserves and cut the bridge to international cooperation by defaulting on its debt, thus turning Peru into a pariah in the financial community.

Peru's top foreign exchange earner during the last decade has been illegal: semipurified paste from coca leaves used in the production of cocaine. Coca has become the most "profitable" crop in a country where agricultural production has grown only half as fast as the population in the past twenty years, at a terrible cost to society. Social turmoil, drug trafficking, and terrorist subversion have contributed to widespread violence, causing 25,000 deaths since 1980; total damages from terrorist actions are estimated at more than $20 billion in the past decade.[6]

According to public opinion polls, by the end of García's government three of every four Peruvians believed their country to be in a state of advanced decay.[7] More than 200,000 people a year, almost 1 percent of the population, have been packing up, selling whatever they can, and emigrating to the United States, Spain, Canada, and other Latin American countries—legally or illegally.

The 1990 Elections

The failures of Alan García's government left a vacuum in Peruvian politics prior to the 1990 presidential elections. Mario Vargas Llosa, the internationally acclaimed novelist, had been acting like a candidate since 1988 and was the acknowledged front-runner until the first-round elections in April 1990. He had stepped into the national political limelight in July 1987 by opposing García's unsuccessful attempt to nationalize the private banking system. Vargas Llosa was supported by a coalition of center-rightist parties called the United Democratic Front (FREDEMO).

Vargas Llosa campaigned on a market oriented platform and was strongly committed to an orthodox austerity program including the elimination of most controls and the full privatization of state-owned enterprises. Eight weeks before the election, Alfonso Barrantes of the Socialist Left was believed to be his closest rival.[8] But Vargas Llosa's incisive criticism of García's party, APRA, and of all Marxist left-wing groups such as those represented by Barrantes, polarized public opinion. Though he was the candidate with the most support, Vargas Llosa also had the most vehement detractors: his opposition easily convinced much of the public that he represented the interests of the traditional ruling classes. The increasingly strident anti–Vargas Llosa campaign, run mainly by the government, led many people to doubt the need for an economic approach as radical as FREDEMO's.

By March, despite the García government's failure, APRA's candidate had dislodged Barrantes from second place in the polls. Meanwhile, a diligent campaign by a tiny new political party named Cambio 90 (Change 90) was beginning to draw attention to its then almost unknown candidate, Alberto Fujimori. Fujimori's campaign slogan, well attuned to the voters' mood, summed up his assets: "Honesty, Technology, and Hard Work." He capitalized on the prestige of the Japanese as an industrious people and implied that Japan could help Peru solve its crisis. Fujimori also benefited from his own image as a center-moderate, from the García government's effective negative campaign against Vargas Llosa, and from alliances with the proselytizing evangelical Christian movement, small businessmen, and entrepreneurs in the informal economy.

His support increasing almost exponentially over the campaign's final three weeks, Fujimori achieved an unprecedented feat in the political history of Latin America. In the April 8 elections, Fujimori came close to beating Vargas Llosa, winning 24.6 percent of the votes to Vargas Llosa's 27.6 percent and forcing a runoff election.

Vargas Llosa was the first to acknowledge that APRA and left-wing support would logically go to Fujimori. Between the first and second rounds, Fujimori attempted to rally round him any economists, politicians, and technicians he thought could convert his main ideas into a government program that looked clearly different from Vargas Llosa's. Vargas Llosa, for his part, tried to improve his image among the poor by emphasizing the social programs that his government would enact. Ethnic and religious confrontations made for a tense electoral climate. Many well-established Peruvian nisei (descendants of Japanese immigrants) who were afraid of a failure by Fujimori, as well as representatives of the Catholic hierarchy who were put off by Fujimori's political connection to evangelist leaders, actively supported Vargas Llosa, a white of Spanish descent and a declared agnostic.

In the official count, Fujimori won 56.5 percent of the votes in the June 10 runoff; Vargas Llosa, 33.9 percent. Cambio 90's triumph swept virtually the whole country, while FREDEMO won victories only in Peru's main jungle city of Iquitos and among Peruvians living abroad.

The New Government

Before taking office, Fujimori was invited by U.N. Secretary General Javier Pérez de Cuéllar to meet with the leaders of multilateral organizations. His trip culminated in Japan, where he expected that his heritage could help him gain some support. The land of his ancestors welcomed him warmly but also gave him some pointed advice: before even thinking of any financial support from Japan, Peru should seek to restore its ties to the international financial community by beginning to repay its multilateral foreign debt and by drawing up its economic policy in concert with the International Monetary Fund (IMF) and the U.S. government. The Japanese government would not wish to add the Peruvian case to the list of grievances between Japan and the United States. It was probably at this point that Fujimori decided on the course his government would take.

Fujimori became convinced that he had to apply a strict, hard-line austerity program—similar to the one he had opposed during the electoral campaign. As his first prime minister and minister of finance, he chose Juan Carlos Hurtado Miller, an acquaintance from university days and a minister of agriculture in the Belaunde government. Hurtado's political background enabled Fujimori to summon a diverse cabinet of technical experts from several political groups. This included representatives from the left, who later resigned over personal differences with the president and the severity of his program.

The economic program announced by Hurtado with Fujimori's blessing initially brought impressive results. Hurtado appeared on television on August 8, 1990, to present an economic "shock" plan that included raising gasoline prices by 3000 percent. Inflation during August alone hit almost 400 percent. But the subsequent drop in demand, along with the cutoff of subsidies and elimination of the fiscal deficit by September, resulted in much lower inflation. Production soon began to recover upon a sounder base.

Fujimori's limited political experience resulted in some gaps in his program and conflicts within his government. As a result of poor fiscal management, Hurtado had to propose in December another rise in the price of fuel, a main source of revenue for the government. A month later, with inflation rebounding, Hurtado could no longer count on general backing from members of his own cabinet, some of whom wanted to roll back the clock and restore some subsidies and controls.

In an effort to save the key aspects of his program, Hurtado resigned in February 1991. Fujimori, instead of heeding Hurtado's critics, summoned Carlos Boloña, an even more committedly orthodox economist than Hurtado, to be his next finance minister.

President Fujimori's First Year in Office

Peru's economy has been radically transformed in the year and a half since Fujimori took office. After years of decline, GDP in 1991 increased by almost 3 percent. Inflation has slowed from its frenetic pace under the previous government to less than 4 percent a month (140 percent for 1991 as a whole against 7,650 percent in 1990), and should continue to fall in 1992.

This progress has been achieved under a price system that has become one of the freest in South America. In addition to ending most subsidies and controls, the government has drastically lowered import barriers. Until July 1990, imports had been subject to 56 different tariffs averaging 66 percent. At least 536 imports were simply prohibited. This system has been replaced by two import tariffs (15 and 25 percent) averaging 17 percent. Almost all tariff-related restrictions have been removed, and the list of prohibited imports has been abolished.

Paralleling its anti-inflation efforts, the government has started to deregulate, liberalize, and privatize to increase competition and economic efficiency. All state-owned monopolies have been eliminated, and state-owned shares in some companies have been transferred to private ownership. New market-oriented laws have been enacted for almost every sector of production, deregulating most industries. The labor market has been made more flexible; for example, new regulations allow the dismissal of workers hired after July 28, 1990 (previous contracts are still protected by the constitutional right to labor stability). The land market has been liberalized. Fujimori has also worked to strengthen relations with neighboring countries to create a climate of trust in the region. On a recent official visit to Ecuador, he proposed to resolve a boundary dispute that has strained relations between the two countries for the past three decades. He also has provided landlocked Bolivia with access to a Pacific Ocean port for its trade.

Fujimori has enacted legislation to stimulate foreign investment, the most important being that foreign capital now receives the same treatment as domestic capital. The first fruits of the reforms are new prospecting contracts signed with foreign oil companies. Mobil Corporation is currently exploring the petroleum potential of the Huallaga basin, and Shell Oil is considering the possibility of investing in the Camisea gasfields, the largest in Latin America. Latin American investors—mainly from Chile, Argentina, and Venezuela—are interested in taking over Peruvian companies that fail to adjust to the new competitive environment. They also want to participate in joint ventures with Peruvians in agroindustry, mining, fishing, and textiles—areas where Peru may have an international competitive advantage. The market seems to confirm these approaches. The average price of industrial companies on the Lima stock exchange almost doubled in the last quarter of 1991.

Despite these improvements, however, numerous problems remain. Fiscal revenue is still too low to cover the state's minimum operating costs, leaving many potential investors skeptical about the medium-term success of the stabilization program. In an effort to raise revenue and reform the tax system, the government has simplified and reduced the number of taxes, eliminating most exemptions. Although some nuisance taxes (like one on bank checks) are still assessed because they are easy to collect, Peru's tax system is much more attractive than it was. But overall, an enormous amount of time and effort will have to be dedicated to combating tax evasion. External balances have improved somewhat, though this is due mainly to repatriation of money that had been held abroad to escape hyperinflation.

The government has started to cut the state payroll, which swelled by 40 percent under García. But the fiscal shortfall has already reduced the average salary in the public sector to $50 a month. Little has been done to improve this situation, which has generated violent demonstrations by schoolteachers, doctors, and other civil servants.

In a suddenly liberalized financial market, the understandable skepticism about the eventual success of the stabilization program has kept interest rates high (6 percent a month in real terms in December 1991). One result of these high rates, along with a big dip in inflation, was a quick recovery of dollar reserves by an average of $100 million a month in the first half of 1991. In an economy that at the time Fujimori took office had a total domestic money supply of only $730 million, this promptly lowered the value of the dollar versus the new sol. As a result, Lima has become the most expensive city in Latin America in terms of dollars. Each U.S. dollar would have to be worth almost 50 percent more soles to make Lima's cost of living comparable to those of cities in neighboring countries. So wide a misalignment, unfortunately, can only be corrected gradually. Agriculture, mining, and Peru's other main export industries are bound to suffer significantly in the short term from the overvalued currency.

With most of the needed laws and regulations now in place, the remaining steps to restore investor confidence will call on the managerial capacity of the government. Only about $3 million has been earned until now from the sale of state-owned assets and companies. Negotiations on foreign debt have moved forward but slowly; not until September 1991 did the government nominate an official debt negotiation committee. The scarcity of good managers has also impeded the implementation of social support programs to relieve poverty.

Beyond the economic crisis, Peruvians are still not sure whether their most basic institutions—the police, the judiciary, social security, education, and regional government—are too corrupt for rehabilitation. Some emergency aid to the poorest people is imperative. As for the 300 deaths a month from political violence, the government still lacks any comprehensive strategy to fight the subversion. Action on all these fronts is essential to restoring confidence in Peru's future.

As of January 1992, President Fujimori enjoyed the support of 65 percent of the people. This is surprising considering he has implemented an orthodox and courageous austerity program that has eliminated all subsidies, reduced both real wages and social expenditures, and initiated the dismissal of public sector workers. To retain this margin of approval, Fujimori has huge hurdles to overcome: defeating inflation once and for all; further refining the state's role in the economy;

restoring a minimum social contract between the state and its citizens; winning the war against terrorism; and giving the poor some reason to have hope for the future. And, of course, these tasks depend on progress in other areas: containing the population explosion; increasing productivity in the rural sector; convincing the young that democracy and well-being are compatible and feasible—even in Peru, a disillusioned country, disappointed in utopian dreams of every kind.

Peru and the United States

If Peru is to move beyond its economic and social crises, it will need the full cooperation of the United States government and of the U.S.-dominated multilateral lending institutions. The United States has for decades been the foreign power that has most influenced Peruvian politics, a situation that has become dramatically more obvious with the collapse of the Soviet Union. Both Europe and Japan trade widely with Peru, but both have shown reluctance to become substantially involved politically anywhere in Latin America. Therefore, the United States has a major role in determining Peru's future.

At a short meeting at the White House in September 1991, President Fujimori and President George Bush reviewed the respective priorities of their countries in the bilateral relationship. For the United States, the main publicly stated issues are drug trafficking and the protection of human rights in Peru's war against subversion. Peru's top priority is, of course, economic recovery, which is seen as a prerequisite to the survival of democracy and to a successful end to the war against the Shining Path. It is essential to see how all three—the devastated economy, drug trafficking, and the guerrilla war—are intimately linked to one another.

The Economic Challenge

The García administration's default on debt cost Peru dearly. Development projects are paralyzed, foreign investment is almost nil, some creditor countries have restricted trade, and financial aid flows are down from previous years. Although García's default made the cutoffs inevitable and necessary, the continuing moratorium on aid and new loans and the emphasis on debt repayment only makes the situation worse. Increasing poverty and collapsing social services help both to inspire the Shining Path and to make the state more vulnerable to drug traffickers. Each of these, in turn, only furthers the damage to the economy. The Shining Path causes billions of dollars in damage every year, hinders business, and chases away investors. Coca dollars, on the other hand, destabilize the exchange rate and distort the economy of whole regions of the country.

The debt crisis dates to 1985, when García began to limit loan payments. Peru was declared ineligible for IMF lending in August 1986 and was put on "nonaccrual" status by the World Bank in 1987 and by the Inter-American Development Bank (IDB) in early 1989. After a warning that continued delinquency would jeopardize its membership in the IMF, García renewed current debt service payments to the IMF in September 1989.

In October 1990, without asking anything in return Fujimori resumed payments of current obligations to the World Bank and the IDB. Debt service payments to the three multilateral institutions amount to some $45 million a month, a sixth of Peru's fiscal revenues. This imposed a major cost on the Peruvian people considering their unfulfilled social needs.

Pending arrears with the IDB were cleared by September 1991. Agreements with the World Bank and the IMF require that accumulated arrears ($1.8 billion) be cleared by December 1992. Peru hopes to finance these payments with loans from a group of creditor countries led by the United States and Japan and from the multilateral lenders themselves, in addition to its own resources.

For the financing to come through, however, the Peruvian government must comply with the fiscal and monetary targets set for 1992 in coordination with the IMF. The radical structural reforms required by the IDB and the World Bank are already mostly in place.

Most of Peru's foreign debt, however, is bilateral and is owed to Paris Club creditors, who have also approved a payment plan for 1992. The total debt owed to Paris Club creditors in June 1991 was $7.8 billion. Another $5.9 billion is owed to commercial banks. Peru's total debt exceeds $22 billion. Some 90 percent of this debt remains in arrears, although the lawsuits that resulted from García's default have been dropped in light of the new government's cooperative efforts. The problem is likely to continue, however, because Peru's current poverty means it is unlikely to be able to repay commercial creditors any time soon. Nevertheless, when President Fujimori was sworn in, Peruvian commercial debt traded in the secondary market at 5 cents on the dollar. By September 1991, the price had risen to 15 cents.

Interest on Peru's foreign debt consumes more than 50 percent of yearly export earnings, against the regional average of 23 percent. Peru's total debt amounts to almost 500 percent of annual export earnings, against 285 percent for Latin America as a whole. Sometime before 1995, Peru will have to coherently restructure its debt so as to defer annual reschedulings of at least two-thirds of the current interest.

Obviously, Peru desperately needs the cooperation of its creditors, especially the United States, for its current radical reforms to succeed. And, equally obvious, the sooner the cooperation comes, the better.

Coca Trafficking

Peru is the source of more than half the world's coca leaf which is used as the raw material for cocaine. In recent years, the main interest of the United States, where some 80 percent of the world's cocaine is consumed, in Peru has been to restrict the export of coca. If this policy is pursued too narrowly, however, it could create more problems than it solves.

Semirefined coca paste is now Peru's single top export. Many areas of the Peruvian economy have come to depend on its income and have become increasingly unstable in the process. The inflow of dollars has also corrupted large portions of the state and has come to provide the Shining Path with its single most important source of income.

Peru shares the U.S. interest in combating the coca trade. The problem is that repressive action in coca-growing areas may only strengthen the rebel grip on the population of the coca-growing Huallaga Valley as the poor people who depend on coca's income increasingly come to see the state as an enemy.

Shining Path and Colombian drug traffickers operate an alliance of mutual interest to protect themselves against U.S.–Peruvian antidrug operations in the Huallaga Valley. The Shining Path has perhaps 3,000 trained soldiers in the area and earns an estimated $30–50 million a year from coca-related activities.

The drug barons have also profited from the coca trade at the expense of Peruvian society. They have created in Peru "an underground economy of unemployed migrants, peasants, officials, and criminals . . . contributing to a culture of shake-downs, payoffs, and cynicism."[9]

Coca, a sacred plant for ancient Peruvian civilizations, has long been used in religious ceremonies and as a medium of exchange.[10] It is a habit among much of the native population to chew on the leaves to ward off hunger and fatigue. The plant is a hardy shrub, yielding three to four crops a year with little investment in fertilizers or seeds. Growing coca as a crop in Peru is at present three times more profitable than cacao and oranges, and six times more profitable than bananas.

Data on the cocaine trade are neither precise nor easy to come by, but Peru probably exports about 2,000 tons of coca paste a year. In Colombia, it is transformed into pure cocaine for export to the United States and Europe. However, for every $100 spent in the U.S. market for cocaine produced from Peruvian coca, less than $1 goes to the peasants who grew the plant, and no more than $4 shows up as a Peruvian export. About 90 percent of all income from the cocaine business—grossly estimated at $80 billion annually—remains in the United States.

During the 1980s, the U.S. and Peruvian governments signed several agreements to curtail coca production by prohibiting cultivation and offering peasants technical and financial support for other activities. The results, however, were unsuccessful. Shortly after Fujimori took office, he decided not to renew one such agreement, involving $100 million in annual aid: $40 million for military and police equipment and $60 million in balance of payments support. (By comparison, the U.S. government spends nearly $15 billion a year in its domestic war on drugs.)

After months of negotiations, a new antidrug agreement was signed in May 1991, with essentially the same provisions that Fujimori rejected the year before. One important new element was U.S. acceptance that Peruvian peasants growing coca should not be prosecuted as criminals. An economic replacement for coca growing is to be sought, in recognition that band-aid assistance and enforcement programs will not by themselves cure the drug epidemic. As Lester Pearson observed, "Development is a long, slogging, grinding effort by the people themselves of each country. Aid should help to build a base for independent and self-reliant growth."[11]

Preserving Democracy

Democracy is essential if Peru's economy is to grow on a sound basis. Democracy is also the key to combating the Shining Path, which wants the state to appear repressive and dictatorial. It is essential to realize that Peru is at war, however, in order to fully understand the problems Peru faces in implementing economic reforms and in combating drug trafficking.

Even in urban centers, where democratic practice in Peru is at its liveliest, basic freedoms are threatened by subversion. Peru truly is fighting to protect its integrity as a democratic nation. About 30 percent of its territory and 50 percent of the population live under a state of military emergency, which restricts some constitutional rights.

Democracy without solid institutions is indeed fragile. The Peruvian Congress can no longer legislate efficiently. Courts are swamped by a backlog of cases. Subversion, party politics, and outright corruption often sway judicial decisions. Legitimate antiguerrilla action has proved ineffective in the absence both of an adequate legal framework to deal with terrorist crimes and of a clear-sighted antisubversion strategy. Appallingly, the state itself frequently adopts terrorist tactics in retaliation against the Shining Path and the MRTA.

Through sabotage, selective murder, and "armed strikes," the Shining Path is seeking to create a situation of generalized terror in Peru. Its organization remains clandestine, sectarian, and fanatical. The police, the military, civilian authorities, and foreign development technicians have been its favored targets. The Shining Path has murdered 131 city mayors since 1984, for instance, leaving a power vacuum in local governments. There are no municipal authorities in 461 of Peru's 1,784 voting districts, belonging to 20 of the country's 24 departments.

Shining Path recruits members among young, unemployed high school graduates in the poorest provinces, and has massacred entire rural communities that resisted its incursions. It even attacks legal Marxist parties for "serving bourgeois democracy." Maria Elena Moyano, a courageous, left-wing community leader of Villa El Salvador, one of Lima's poorest areas, was murdered in February 1992, and her body blown to pieces.

In addition to using terrorism, the Shining Path works aggressively to infiltrate the police, the armed forces, labor unions, and political organizations. Peruvian cities are the principal centers for these activities. The Shining Path also has representatives in the main European capitals where information is distributed about their activities.

In contrast to the Shining Path, MRTA actions are more typical of traditional Marxist-Leninist guerrilla movements. It uses social pressure, allegedly to improve the popular welfare. Whereas the Shining Path seeks to replace every vestige of the state, the MRTA tries to force the state to surrender benefits to the people.

Unfortunately, the government is still fighting subversion with mainly military action, whereas the challenge to its authority is political and therefore demands a more political response. The Fujimori administration does seem more aware than earlier governments that it must develop a more coherent and methodical approach to combating subversion. In this fight, respect for basic human rights is essential to win over the poorest Peruvians, whose plight the Shining Path brandishes like a standard to justify violence and terrorism. And, to bring this discussion back to where it began, equally essential as respect for human rights is economic development. Unless people believe the state can provide them with basic necessities, any efforts to keep them out of the Shining Path's hands will likely fail. So one of the most effective ways other governments can help preserve Peruvian democracy is to provide critically needed aid and loans.

Conclusions

The economic policies defined by the Fujimori administration, if managed properly, could reverse Peru's economic and social decline. Right now, fiscal stabilization is the most urgent priority. This requires not only collecting more taxes but also restructuring the state itself, including cutting the size of public institutions, privatizing public enterprises, and reforming the civil service.

If the government manages to stay on its present course, structural reform could well lift the Peruvian economy out of its slump and help to restore creditworthiness. The timing and intensity of the rewards from pursuing responsible policies are hard to predict, but in just under two years, Peru has already seen hope begin to replace pessimism. In December 1991, 41 percent of the population thought that the economic situation would improve in 1992.[12] The understanding and aid of foreign governments are essential. If structural reform does not succeed and Peru becomes further mired in social and political strife, neighboring countries could be endangered at a time when democracy is being consolidated and free markets developed throughout the region. As has always been the case, whatever happens to Peru is bound to reverberate throughout the region as a whole.

Notes

1. President Fujimori's father first set foot in Peru in the 1920s to work on a cotton plantation. He returned briefly to Japan to find a wife, starting a family in 1934. He set up a small business which was seized during World War II.

Like his brothers and sisters, Alberto Fujimori went to a public high school in Lima. In 1960, he graduated as an agronomist from Peru's National Agricultural University at La Molina. He was an honors student with a special capacity for rational analysis. He won scholarships that enabled him to attend American and European universities for graduate work in mathematics.

He returned to his alma mater, La Molina, as a professor of calculus. Unlike the majority of the hardworking nisei in Peru, who have traditionally kept a low profile in Peruvian society, Fujimori was open about his ambitions and interested in gaining public exposure. In 1980, he attempted unsuccessfully to set himself up as candidate for a seat in Congress. He later showed strong political instincts by climbing the academic ladder to become president of the Agricultural University, and eventually president of the National Assembly of University Presidents.

However, the main springboard for Fujimori's candidacy was not his bureaucratic tenure at La Molina but a television program he started, entitled "Concertando," which was shown weekly on the state-owned network during most of President Alan García's tenure. It was evident that Fujimori was looking for some role in national politics. However, when he started his political campaign everyone, including his wife, thought that he was aspiring to be elected as a senator. (Peruvian electoral law allows a presidential candidate to run simultaneously for the Senate, thus permitting greater exposure for representatives of small parties or independent groups.)

The presidency has changed Fujimori very little. He still works twelve to thirteen hours a day and takes his youngest son Kenji fishing some weekends. When elected, Fujimori knew little about the everyday tasks of the presidency, but he has been learning fast on the job. His rational mind and methodical approach are suited to a bureaucratic administrative style, though he is not altogether devoid of audacity. Sometimes slow to make decisions, he can be authoritarian in enforcing them. He delegates little. His best qualities are his pragmatism and an iron will. A Lima joke calls his mind "a strange combination of Japanese hardware and Peruvian software."

2. Economic data for the period 1950–1990 have been taken from the Instituto Nacional de Estadística, *Perú: Compendio Estadístico 1990–91* (Lima, 1990). Estimates for 1991 have been calculated by APOYO, S. A.

3. For a historical review of Peruvian debt to 1987, see Felipe Ortiz de Zevallos, *The Peruvian Puzzle* (New York: Priority Press Publications, 1989).

4. "Desarrollar la Guerra Popular Sirviendo a la Revolución Mundial," a Shining Path document signed in August 1986.

5. "La Reforma Económica Estructural con Base en el Mercado: Un Estudio Internacional," a study prepared by the Futures Group for the Center for International Private Enterprise, Glastonbury, England, 1991.

6. "Informe de la Comisión Especial de Investigación y Estudio sobre la Violencia y Alternativas de Pacificación del Senado de la República," (Report) Lima, 1989.

7. APOYO, S. A., public opinion poll, Lima, January 1990. The poll was based on interviews with 600 people representative of the population of Lima.

8. Ibid.

9. Edmundo Morales, *Cocaine: White Gold Rush in Peru* (Tucson: University of Arizona Press, 1989), p. xvi. This is an in-depth analysis of coca production in the Peruvian Andes.

10. Recognizing coca's cultural significance for the Indian population, the Peruvian government established the Empresa Nacional de la Coca (ENACO) almost a century ago as a public enterprise to supply coca leaves for traditional uses.

11. Lester B. Pearson, *The Crisis of Development* (New York: Praeger Publishers, 1970).

12. APOYO, S. A., public opinion poll, Lima, December 1991.

PERU: ECONOMIC STATISTICS

	1986	1987	1988	1989	1990	1991e
Domestic Economy						
Real GDP (% change)	9.2	8.5	-8.3	-11.6	-4.9	3.0
Per capita GDP (1990 US$)[1]	1,169	1,242	1,115	965	900	927
Per capita real GDP (% change)	6.9	6.2	-10.2	-13.4	-6.8	0.6
Inflation (% change)	63	115	1,722	2,775	7,650	139
Population (millions)	19.8	20.3	20.7	21.1	21.6	22.1
Unemployment (% of labor force)[2]	5.3	4.8	na	7.9	8.3	na
Central government deficit (% of GDP)	3.6	5.7	2.5	4.5	2.6	na
Real deposit interest rate	-19.6	-37.8	-84.2	-55.2	-69.8	11.4
Private sector average wages (index 1980=100)						
white collar	97.7	1,01.1	63.0	40.5	31.4	35.3[3]
blue collar	79.1	84.8	54.3	33.3	27.6	27.7[3]
External Economy (US$, millions)						
Official exchange rate (inti-US$)	14	17	129	2,666	187,886	770,833
Parallel exchange rate (inti-US$)	18	40	315	4,395	206,441	774,083
Merchandise exports	2,531	2,661	2,691	3,488	3,276	3,351
Merchandise imports	-2,596	-3,182	-2,790	-2,291	-2,885	-2,956
Trade balance	-65	-521	-99	1,197	391	395
Current account balance	na	-1,890	-1,479	-429	-1,521	-1,600
Total external debt	14,477	15,373	16,493	16,827	17,347	22,642[4]
% of GDP	51.4	52.5	64.2	77.5	89.4	116.8
% of merchandise exports	572.0	277.7	612.9	482.4	529.5	675.7

	1986	1987	1988	1989	1990	1991e
Public debt service[5]	495	422	158	183	240	na
- % of merchandise exports	19.6	15.9	5.9	5.2	7.3	na

e estimate

[1] Estimated by APOYO.
[2] This figure does not accurately reflect the high rate of underemployment in Peru.
[3] As of June 1991.
[4] As of June 1991. Until 1990, Peruvian official statistics did not include imputed interest on arrears which, since 1983, account for a growing percentage of total debt.
[5] The bulk of total debt and of debt service is explained by the public debt.

Source: Instituto Nacional de Estadística

Peru: Average Growth Rates (1951-1990)

	Real GDP	Real per capita GDP	Inflation	Exports	Population
1951-1960	5.7	2.93	7.8	8.5	2.7
1961-1970	5.3	2.34	9.3	5.6	2.9
1971-1980	3.8	1.00	30.3	3.0	2.7
1981-1985	-0.4	-2.67	103.0	1.0	2.3
1986-1990	-1.8	3.82	823.7	-2.6	2.1

Source: Instituto Nacional de Estadística

4 / Venezuela: The Struggle for Reform

Robert Bottome

Venezuela is in the midst of a far-reaching reform process that aims to shift economic activity from government control to free markets, restructuring a costly and inefficient public sector and breaking the power of the political party cliques that have been the main beneficiaries of state capitalism for almost two decades. The success or failure of this reform effort will determine Venezuela's future course, whether it is toward economic progress, which will require greater political pluralism, or economic decay under the guidance of the traditional elites. The outlook is promising, but the old ways are deeply rooted and vested interests are fighting hard to preserve the status quo ante.

For more than sixty years, beginning in the 1920s, Venezuelan society was characterized by a paternalistic government overseeing the distribution of huge oil rents, a pattern that produced one of the most regulated and protected economies on this side of the iron curtain. Politically, it also produced a party system characterized by patronage ("clientelismo"), corruption, and increasing voter alienation and electoral absenteeism. Under this setup, Venezuela enjoyed growth and well-being for many decades but, since the 1970s, the result has been a stagnating economy, an increasingly inefficient public sector, and rapidly deteriorating public services. Additionally, the country got itself into trouble through an excess of foreign debt, forcing it to turn to the international lending institutions for help for the first time.

The author is indebted to Rita Funaro, Robert Bond, and Bruce Fitzgerald for their contributions to this chapter.

In 1989, a new administration broke sharply with the past, introducing measures to open the economy to competition from abroad and to restructure the public sector. The new macroeconomic rules included market-determined prices and interest rates; a floating, competitive exchange rate; and sharply reduced protectionism.

Although the new macroeconomic rules are in place, vested interests are fighting hard to delay or block the reforms. In the second half of 1990, it appeared they might succeed. Higher oil prices caused by the Persian Gulf crisis offered an illusion that the reforms were unnecessary and that Venezuela could revert to its old ways.

But in January 1991, oil prices plummeted and the illusion was punctured. The nation is now in the midst of an intense struggle, with bureaucrats, labor leaders, and party officials arrayed against a small but determined band of reform-minded individuals who are seeking to transform Venezuela's society into one that is democratic, market oriented, and prosperous. In spite of resistance from these vested interests and widespread incomprehension of the government's aims, progress is being made.

The struggle also involves the military and the people. Deteriorating services, rising crime rates, and inflation have buffeted the man on the street, eroding support for the democratic system. The failed putsch of February 4, 1992, represented an attempt by disgruntled junior military officers to take advantage of this erosion to gain power for themselves. That the Venezuelan people, however, did not rally behind the government highlights the need for political reform and improved public services. It also underscores the fact that time is short.

◆ ◆ ◆

Venezuela has completed the first stage of a difficult and traumatic transformation. Remarkable changes were wrought during the first half of Carlos Andrés Pérez's second five-year presidential term, which began in February 1989. After half a century of government control, regulations, paternalism, protectionism, an overvalued exchange rate, and an inward-looking economic development model, Venezuela changed course to become more outwardly oriented, more competitive, and, surprisingly, more democratic. During the second Pérez administration's first year, the macroeconomic rules of the game were changed completely: Most price controls were eliminated. Interest rates were freed to be set by market forces. Exchange controls were scrapped, and the bolivar was floated for the first time ever. Protectionism and import restrictions began to be dismantled. A start was made in efforts to reorganize or privatize state companies and government services.

Profound as the changes were, defining the new macroeconomic rules of the game was the "easy" part. The "hard" part is already under way, but success is far from assured. In order to ensure the permanence of Venezuela's economic and political transformation, the country's governing, administrative, and party institutions must be reformed. This will require organization, drive, and consummate skill to counter the power of those committed to preserving traditional systems of economic and political patronage.

The process will require many years to complete under the best of circumstances. Vested interests have successfully opposed reforms in many areas but are being forced to give ground in other equally important ones. The challenge is to achieve quickly those strategic changes that will ensure the process has enough momentum to prevent its reversal by the next government. Time is short. Gubernatorial and municipal elections are scheduled for December 1992; presidential and congressional elections for 1993.

Until these elections take place, Pérez, a dynamic and charismatic leader who seemingly has the capacity to mobilize public opinion in support of change and thus to overwhelm the resistance of various vested interests, will try to accomplish as much as is feasible. Pérez's present commitment to an open economy and democratic reform contrasts sharply with the state control and interventionism that characterized his first term in office, from 1974 to 1979. Some outside observers suggest that Pérez's thinking was profoundly influenced by the experiences of other countries, notably Alan García's Peru and Felipe González's Spain.

World oil markets will help determine how fast the country mends its ways. Paradoxically, lower oil prices are good news in the context of Venezuelan reform; they promote change by driving home the point that the traditional solutions no longer apply, while higher prices rekindle illusions that Venezuela will be able to spend its way out of its problems.

Lower oil prices alone will not be sufficient to generate the necessary changes, however. Also, the president and his team must be able to communicate the need for reform; without strong public support, resistance to change cannot be overcome.

In part, the failure to develop this communication reflects the administration's inability to achieve political reforms. Venezuelans vote by slate rather than individual ballots, a system that renders elected officials accountable to party officials, not the electorate. More important, the sad state of Venezuela's health, education, transportation, and personal security services is linked in the public mind with "corruption," which, in turn, is part and parcel of "government" and maybe even of "democracy."

Unless corrupt officials are identified and punished, and unless the quality of public services improves, the reform effort, and Venezuela's democratic system, could fail.

Almost as important is inflation. In a country long accustomed to stable prices, inflation rates in recent years have been a source of dismay and confusion. This puts the administration in a bind: the only way to contain inflation is to curb the growth of public sector spending—at a time when increased social spending is a must.

During the remainder of President Pérez's term, significant progress must be made in implementing essential reforms to put Venezuela solidly on the road to global competitiveness. These reforms include, among others, privatizing or reorganizing many state companies and services, introduction of a value-added tax, key labor law amendments, financial system modernization, and ports reorganization. Equally important are proposals to open up the nation's political system to give voters a more direct say in choosing their representatives and to insulate the judicial system from political pressure.

Background

Venezuela is going through its second major transformation in less than a century. The first started in 1922 when an exploratory well on the eastern shore of Lake Maracaibo blew out. One of the most prolific wells in oil history, "Los Barrosos No. 2," is still producing today, sixty-nine years later.

Los Barrosos marked Venezuela's emergence as a major oil producer. By 1928, Venezuela was the world's largest exporter, a position it held for nearly forty years before giving way to the more fruitful Middle Eastern producers.

Rising oil revenues brought many benefits to Venezuela. It also did great harm in two ways that are only now beginning to be understood.

A basic legal principle handed down from colonial times specifies that subsoil wealth does not belong to the surface property holder but to the Crown—or in its stead, the national government. Thus, control of the newfound oil wealth was vested in Venezuela's government. For over half a century, the Venezuelan economy revolved around the government's distribution of huge revenues generated by the oil industry. This structure helps explain why so many sectors of Venezuelan society became so dependent on the central government, and why Venezuelan governments became increasingly paternalistic and repressive.

The organization of Venezuelan society was analogous to a wheel, with the central government at the hub dealing with the different sectors along each of the spokes. The government was the supreme interlocutor in this model. Direct communications between the individual sectors were virtually nonexistent. Each sector negotiated individually with the central government. A business might be granted tariff protection and credit but would have to accept an extraordinary degree of control and regulation in exchange. Labor might benefit from a compulsory wage hike, but its freedom to strike was circumscribed.

The "wheel" eventually encompassed the political system as well. Though nominally a democracy, Venezuela's political system is tightly controlled by small, self-perpetuating cliques. Until recently, the only public official elected by direct popular vote was the president. All others in effect were appointed by the parties' all-powerful executive committees. Venezuelans cast only two votes, one for the president and one for a party.

The state became increasingly powerful. Arturo Uslar Pietri, a leading Venezuelan intellectual and political figure, recently spoke of a "nation that lives off the State" instead of a nation that lives off its production and effort. Oil revenues, he noted, were spent "on the creation of a gigantic bureaucracy, a monstrous State [all in the name of] State capitalism," instead of providing for Venezuela's housing, education, and public health needs.

Oil also did serious harm because it resulted in the bolivar's persistent overvaluation relative to the rest of the economy and contributed to the overprotected nature of the nonoil economy. The bolivar's exchange rate was set in terms of the highly profitable oil industry but was overvalued in terms of nonoil activities. The oil industry could easily cover Venezuela's foreign exchange requirements regardless of the performance of the local economy. The currency's overvaluation encouraged imports at the expense of internal economic development, hurting the competitiveness of local industry. An elaborate system of multiple exchange rates, licenses, prohibitions, investment controls, tariffs, and price controls evolved to protect local manufacturers and employment.

As long as oil wealth grew, the overly protected, controlled, and grotesquely inefficient economy was not a political or social issue. The old system produced many benefits. Although income distribution was skewed, Venezuela's standard of living was among the highest in Latin America. Life expectancies increased from under fifty years in the 1920s to over seventy today. The average Venezuelan is four to six inches taller than his parents. Illiteracy was reduced.

Sometime during the past twenty years, however, the old model lost its viability. Since 1974, successive governments have borrowed or drawn down the nation's international reserves to increase spending, but that spending failed to produce lasting growth. On the contrary, gross domestic product (GDP) per capita fell by more than 1 percent per year from 1974 through 1988 while the quality of public services deteriorated, leaving most Venezuelans worse off economically and socially than before the 1970s oil boom. One startling statistic indicates that the old model is no longer functioning: In 1955, Venezuela's nonoil GDP per capita was equivalent to 38 percent of the total for the United States. At the time, it was thought Venezuela would catch up with the United States within forty or fifty years. But the country lost ground instead; in 1990, its nonoil GDP per capita was only 15 percent of that of the United States (see Figure 1).

By 1989, the nation was also deeply in debt. In the 1970s and early 1980s, successive governments borrowed more than $25 billion abroad. Including the private sector, the total owed increased tenfold in fifteen years, from $3 billion in 1973 to $33–35 billion in 1988. Health and literacy standards began to deteriorate as government-provided medical and education services became increasingly corrupt and inefficient. Infrastructure began to deteriorate due to inadequate maintenance. In the 1970s, Caracas boasted the best water system on the continent; today, service interruptions are common. Similarly, the telephone service, once the envy of the continent, has deteriorated dramatically. The completion rate for calls is around 30 percent, and the average waiting time for a new phone is now eight years.

The system's capacity to adjust and renew itself was increasingly compromised by a political system that concentrated power in the hands of a few party officials. In 1958, following the overthrow of military dictator Marcos Pérez Jiménez, Venezuela's democratic leaders, mindful that earlier experiments with radical social and economic reform had led to the reinstitution of military dictatorship, made compromise and incremental change their watchwords. The leaders of the political

VENEZUELA: THE STRUGGLE FOR REFORM • 65

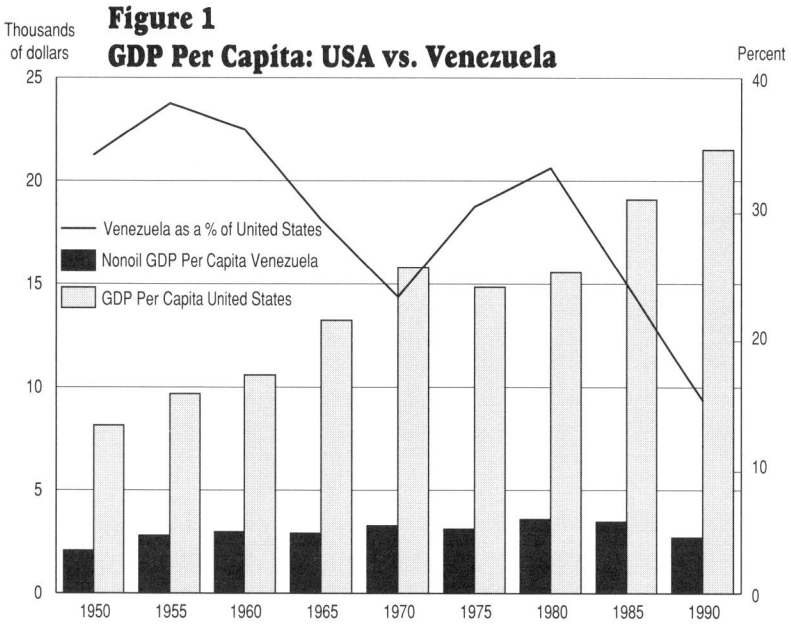

Figure 1
GDP Per Capita: USA vs. Venezuela

- Venezuela as a % of United States
- Nonoil GDP Per Capita Venezuela
- GDP Per Capita United States

Source: IMF, Central Bank and VenEconomy estimates

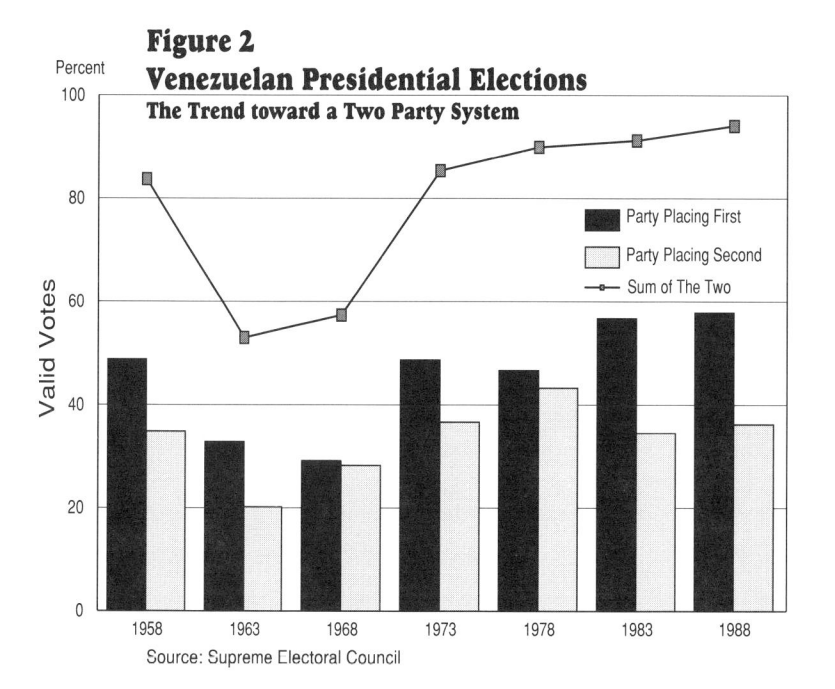

Figure 2
Venezuelan Presidential Elections
The Trend toward a Two Party System

- Party Placing First
- Party Placing Second
- Sum of The Two

Source: Supreme Electoral Council

parties in 1958 signed a preelectoral agreement to share positions in the new government, and a decisionmaking system evolved that featured compromise, bargaining, and extensive consultation among leaders of key groups. Petroleum wealth aided the process, providing resources to satisfy at least some of the demands of competing groups: the military, labor, business, the middle class, peasants, and the urban poor.

For two decades, Venezuelan politics has been dominated by two political parties, social democratic Acción Democrática (AD) and social Christian Copei. Originally representing differing ideologies and social groups, these two parties have become markedly similar in their ideologies and appeals to the electorate, each trying to grab the center of the political spectrum. As socialist politician José Vicente Rangel said in the early 1970s, "Choosing between AD and Copei is like choosing between Pepsi-Cola and Coke." Figure 2 illustrates the degree to which AD and Copei control political power.

The country's electoral system reinforces the hold of these two parties over politics and public policymaking. Until 1989, only the president was elected by direct popular vote. State governors were appointed by the president. All other officeholders (members of Congress, state legislators, and municipal councilors) were elected indirectly via a party list system. This vested control of the political system in the hands of a few politicians in each party: an "elected" official is accountable to his party's executive committee instead of the voter. The parties have a vertical structure and strict internal discipline, which further concentrates power, enabling executive committee members to perpetuate themselves in power. Over time, the system became increasingly unresponsive—and corrupt.

This party and electoral system served Venezuela well in the 1960s, when several competing, ideologically distinct parties offered voters a choice. Also, at the time Venezuela's major parties had capable, honest, and ideologically motivated leaders. Over the past two decades, however, the duopoly status of the two largest parties, the trivialization of left and right, and the breakdown of consensus within the parties on social and economic goals has produced fragmentation, corruption, and disarray.

To a significant degree, AD and Copei have become patronage machines that view elections as essential to continuing the spoils system, rather than political organizations dedicated to implementing social and economic programs. State capitalism came to be seen not as a method for promoting economic development or distributing more equitably the results of economic growth but as a means for political cliques to entrench themselves in power and reap financial rewards. All too often, corrupt politicians were neither punished by the judicial system nor disciplined by their parties.

Voting patterns reflected the population's growing disenchantment with the parties. In the 1973 presidential election, over 96 percent of the electorate voted. Despite the fact that voting is mandatory in Venezuela, in 1988 only 82 percent voted, and of these, 4 percent cast "null" votes, mostly as a form of protest. And, in the 1989 gubernatorial and municipal election, the first of its kind, only 42 percent bothered to cast valid votes.

Pressure for change has been growing since the early 1980s. The Roraima Group, an association of young businessmen and professionals, produced an in-depth study in 1983–84 that called for less control and regulation, a competitive exchange rate, and a more representative democracy. These proposals were expanded by the State Reform Commission (Copre). However, they were ignored until 1989 by a political sector determined to conserve its privileges and ascendancy. Pressure for change was also resisted by many businessmen and labor leaders who had benefited from the traditional closed economic system, which preserved high wages for a labor elite and assured protected industries' profitability. Moreover, as has now become evident, the old ways were deeply rooted in the nation's culture, customs, and law. In this sense, it is almost as difficult to open the Venezuelan economy, notwithstanding the existence of an enterprise culture, as it is to reform and democratize the economy of a nation like Hungary or Poland.

Jaime Lusinchi, Venezuela's president from 1984 until early 1989, will be remembered for his failure to promote change when macroeconomic conditions were easier and the process could have been more gradual and less painful for the country. Lusinchi's administration came to power about the time when foreign banks, reeling from Mexico's declaration of its inability to meet interest payments on its debt in 1982, were abandoning their free and easy lending policies and were frantically trying to reduce their Latin American exposure. The debt crisis signified that Venezuela was no longer able to borrow abroad to finance additional spending at home. But instead of forcing government to cut back, it simply led the administration to experiment with other, more inflationary means to finance expenditures. From 1986 through 1988, Lusinchi embarked on a reckless strategy of seeking growth through increased public spending at a time when oil revenues were falling.

In a sense, Lusinchi's strategy was successful. The economy grew slightly, and he left office as a popular president. This growth carried with it an extraordinary cost, however. Venezuela's long tradition as a low-inflation country was shattered when prices rose 90 percent in the final two years of Lusinchi's term (1987–88). The public sector deficit reached the equivalent of nearly 10 percent of gross domestic product. And 80 percent of the country's international reserves were squandered in just three years, as oil prices fell more than 46 percent. Lusinchi emptied the till and bankrupted Venezuela.

The Reform Process Begins

When Carlos Andrés Pérez assumed the presidency, the fast-developing economic crisis made change inevitable, but hardly anyone was prepared for the profound reforms he introduced in just a few months. In spite of the longest and most expensive political campaign in the country's history, very little was said to inform the voters about the nature and extent of Venezuela's economic peril. Rather, AD's Carlos Andrés Pérez and Copei's Eduardo Fernández tried to outdo each other in promising a continuing flow of benefits to organized labor, the middle class, and groups whose support at the margin could make the difference in the election. As a result, as 1989 dawned there appeared to be widespread popular support in Venezuela for the traditional interventionist model. All outward signs pointed to a continuation of the policies of the past.

To his credit, President Pérez recognized that state spending fueled by oil revenues and external borrowing would no longer produce painless economic growth. The new administration proceeded to define and implement a new development model, with support from the World Bank and IMF, and is apparently committed to maintaining this strategy until President Pérez leaves office in February 1994. (Venezuelan presidents cannot serve two consecutive terms.) If the strategy succeeds, the rules of the game and the institutional framework for doing business in Venezuela will have been changed forever.

The new administration's plans were given an unexpected boost by a sudden development: on February 27–28, 1989, many of Venezuela's poor participated in widespread riots and looting of stores and supermarkets throughout the nation. The riots caught all observers by surprise, and even today, there is considerable disagreement about their cause and significance. Like the Watts riots in Los Angeles or the 1968 Paris uprising, the riots clearly were a watershed event. In retrospect, it appears the riots resulted from the pent-up frustrations accumulated from a decade of economic stagnation, deteriorating public services, and increasing corruption. Many factors contributed, including anxiety about pending price increases and a looming recession, a yellow press and alarmist radio commentary, deliberate provocation by extremist groups, and the government's lack of preparation and complacency. Ill-timed bus fare increases triggered the riots themselves, but higher bus fares were not the real reason for the riots any more than high temperatures were the reason for the "long hot summer" in the United States. The riots served to alert all Venezuelans to the fact that all was not well, that the Lusinchi administration's "prosperity" was an illusion, and that reforms were necessary.

The impression exists outside Venezuela that the riots were triggered by an IMF program. That view is incorrect: the agreement with the IMF was signed on February 28, one day after the rioting had begun.

In the months following the riots, exchange controls were eliminated and multiple rates unified. The bolivar was devalued from 14.50 to the dollar in March to 43 to the dollar in December and to 60 to the dollar by August 1991. The exchange rate is now set by world markets with limited intervention by the Central Bank, instead of by government fiat. Price controls were eliminated for all but eighteen categories of goods that represented less than 8 percent of consumption; the list has since been pared to just three items and will be eliminated in 1992. Interest rates are now being set by market forces and are positive in real terms for the first time in more than a decade.

Venezuela's pervasive protectionist barriers are being torn down. Most prior licenses and other nontariff barriers have been eliminated. The maximum tariff was set at 80 percent in June 1989. It was lowered to 50 percent in March 1990 and to 40 percent in March 1991. The original plan called for further reductions of 10 percent per year to a level of 20 percent in March 1993. However, the 20 percent rate was applied in February 1992, fourteen months ahead of schedule. Moreover, tariffs are being reduced to zero during 1992 for all trade within the Andean region, which comprises Bolivia, Colombia, Ecuador, Peru, and Venezuela. Additionally, Venezuela has entered into or is negotiating trade agreements with Chile, Argentina, Mexico, Central America and the Caribbean, and the United States. Venezuela acceded to the General Agreement on Tariffs and Trade (GATT) in mid-1990.

A new foreign investment regime was adopted whereby virtually all barriers were eliminated. In most fields, a foreign investor is now accorded exactly the same rights and obligations as a domestic investor. Most of the exceptions have, or will be, dealt with via legislative amendments. Venezuela's income tax, for instance, now compares favorably with that of most other countries: the maximum corporate and personal rate is now 30 percent instead of 50 percent. Dividends are now tax free. Progress may prove slower in other areas, however. The bank lobby, for instance, has thus far blocked proposals to open that sector to investment from abroad.

Subsidy policies have been completely overhauled. In the past, governments would subsidize local producers directly via cash payments or indirectly via a favorable exchange rate. Government companies would also buy crops from farmers at one price for resale to processors at lower prices. The result was a wasteful system that produced few benefits for the poor but many opportunities for graft among those who paid the subsidies, allocated preferred-rate dollars, or participated in the lucrative cross-border smuggling of low-price Venezuelan consumer products to Colombia, the Caribbean islands, and other nearby locations. The Pérez administration scrapped the traditional subsidies, replacing them with a system whereby the poor now receive payments in cash and in kind worth approximately one-half the minimum wage. Though the new system is almost as paternalistic as its predecessor, it at least has the virtues of being more efficient while permitting farm product and consumer prices to seek their own free market level.

The 1989 economic measures were designed to eliminate severe economic distortions and lay the macroeconomic groundwork for a new, different Venezuela. Although 1989 was one of the most difficult years in the nation's history, both goals were achieved.

The economy contracted 8.6 percent in 1989, while inflation was a record 81 percent and unemployment rose from 7 to 11 percent. However, the accumulated distortions of many years were worked out of the system, and the bases were laid for renewed growth under rules to make the economy more productive and efficient. Moreover, Venezuela's international accounts were brought into balance with a modest current account surplus, a marked improvement over 1988's record deficit of $5.8 billion.

The new administration also initiated political reform, designed to make the parties more democratic and elected officials accountable to the electorate for their actions. For instance, despite resistance by both major parties, state governors and mayors were elected directly for the first time in the state and municipal elections held in December 1989. The change could have profound long-term effects: these governors and mayors are the first Venezuelan public officials that are fully accountable to the electorate, mandated to present themselves to the voters again in the December 1992 regional elections. (Since he cannot succeed himself, the president is not accountable to the electorate.)

1990: The Spotlight on Institutional Reform

The Pérez administration's most difficult challenge is to reorganize and restructure the state. Service delivery, as mentioned previously, is wasteful and inadequate. Until recently, there was no "safety net" for dealing with the problems of the critically poor, who were instead dependent on the patronage benefits that managed to trickle down to them. The state also owns and operates hundreds of companies, ranging from steel mills to racetracks, almost all of which are persistent money losers. Moreover, the government's revenue base is too narrow. The oil industry generates taxes and royalties equivalent to 19–22 percent of GDP. Government revenues from all other sources represent only 9–11 percent of GDP, however, compared with 25–35 percent in most other countries. In 1989, many analysts assumed that if the Perez/IMF macroeconomic program was maintained, market forces would inevitably compel progress in terms of institutional change, with loss-making state companies being restructured or sold and inefficient public services reorganized. In 1990, however, it become increasingly clear that market forces alone cannot compel the kind of structural reform that Venezuela requires. The interests—political, labor, and business—that have controlled these institutions for decades and derived economic and political power from them through the exercise of clientelismo are deeply entrenched.

Until recently, the opposition parties relied primarily on negative rhetoric, trying to argue that the reforms are not really necessary or paying lip service to the stated goals while promoting legislation to gut the program. Even the president's own party, Acción Democrática, has openly opposed the administration's program. However, none offered any alternatives to the program they wanted to sink. Many government officials and bureaucrats appeared to be opposed. The Venezuelan Workers Confederation (CTV) openly sabotaged administration initiatives in the Congress and in the media. And many businessmen lobbied for a return to protectionism and subsidies.

It became evident that the Pérez administration was not prepared to engage in frontal conflict with any of these groups. The president clearly believes he will gain more through his powers of persuasion and patronage, plus pressure from public opinion, than he would by formally breaking with his party. Despite presidential announcements at the end of 1989 that the program would be continued and intensified in 1990, the first part of the year was a stalemate. There was much discussion of what additional measures were necessary but few decisions. Debate swirled around such issues as gasoline prices, transportation policy, privatization, and agricultural reform, but there was no forward movement. This led to mounting criticism of the administration, with some analysts openly speculating that President Pérez had lost his commitment to keep his program on track.

At midyear, there were signs that these critics had been too quick in condemning the government's inaction. The issue of gasoline prices was finally settled sensibly, with prices at the pump increased in 4–5 percent monthly increments, from 20 cents a gallon at midyear to around 28 cents at year end. A transportation policy was announced that recognized sharply higher fares were needed to generate the cash flow to renew the nation's aging vehicle and aircraft stock. The young technocrat who designed that policy was appointed minister of transport and communications with a mandate to carry it out and to institute reforms in key areas affecting business, including the ports, the merchant marine, the state telephone monopoly, and the state-owned airlines. Two of Venezuela's most qualified executives were named to head CANTV, the state telecommunications monopoly, and Viasa, the state-owned international airline, both with a mandate to privatize those entities as quickly as possible.

The agriculture sector was finally brought into the program. A capable manager who believes in reform was appointed minister of agriculture. Import licenses have been phased out for most farm products. Tariff rates of 10–40 percent, depending on the degree of transformation, are being reduced to 10–20 percent, in tandem with manufactured products. Special regimens have or are being developed for seven items considered "sensitive" or whose world prices are subject to severe distortions: animal feed, corn, milk, oilseeds, rice, sugar, and wheat. These items comprise approximately 60 percent of Venezuelan agricultural production.

The administration began to lobby hard for broad-ranging income tax reform and for a value-added tax (VAT). It pressed ahead with plans for a wholesale restructuring of the financial sector, including redefining the roles of the regulatory and monetary authorities, promoting greater competition within the system, and eliminating most of the barriers to foreign investment in the field.

It appeared the administration was following a well-thought-out strategy, concentrating its efforts in a few critical areas and relying on successes in those areas to generate support for broader reform later on. The outlook for the new economic program started to improve. Though the old guard continued to oppose the reforms, younger leaders were beginning to realize that the old ways were no longer viable and that the changes would be beneficial in the medium and longer terms.

At mid-year, a breakthrough was achieved on the nation's foreign debt. The Pérez administration had inherited a huge foreign debt burden: $34.7 billion at year-end 1988, of which $26.3 billion was owed by the public sector and more than half was either past due or scheduled for payment in 1989–90. Interest payments alone represented over 25 percent of export earnings.

Venezuela's debt was less of a problem than it would have appeared at first glance. Internal, bolivar-denominated public debt was relatively modest, totaling an estimated 200 billion bolivars, equivalent to approximately ten percent of GDP. Though its $2,000 per capita foreign debt was one of the highest of any debtor nation, Venezuela's debt was less of a burden by most other measures. With $10–12 billion per year of exports, Venezuela's problems were primarily those of restructuring the maturity profile of its borrowings to make repayment, and not a fundamental inability to pay.

Moreover, Venezuela was in the enviable position of having virtually no debts with international agencies such as the IMF, World Bank, and Inter-American Development Bank. Those entities were willing to lend up to $10 billion over five years to help finance the transition to a more open and competitive economy.

In 1989 and early 1990, the debt constituted a powerful stimulus for reform: the new administration's access to credit was in effect conditioned on its ability to stick with the program. Debt was also a drag on the administration, however, since negotiating it occupied the time of many senior policy officials and distracted them from other economic issues.

In August 1990, the nation's commercial bank creditors subscribed to a voluntary plan to reduce and restructure some $20 billion worth of past-due or soon-to-mature debt. The affected debt will now be paid over seven to twenty years. In round numbers, the agreement saved $1.7 billion (57 percent) in net debt service in its first year and somewhat less in each succeeding year.

August 1990: The Oil Mirage Appears

Just as its institutional reform strategy was fully defined, the Pérez administration's commitment to reform was put to a severe test: Iraq invaded Kuwait and oil prices doubled. Crying "God is a Venezuelan," old-line interest groups and lobbies immediately redoubled pressures to dilute or reverse the administration's policies.

Although some technocrats continued to work steadfastly to advance the reforms, the government in general was content to rest on its laurels and allow the increased inflow of oil revenues to drive the economy toward better-than-expected results for the year.

Venezuela's GDP grew 5.3 percent in 1990, thanks to a 3.7 percent climb in nonoil GDP—and an extraordinary 13.6 percent jump in oil GDP. Inflation, reflecting measures taken in the previous year, totaled 36.5 percent for the year, compared with 81 percent in 1989. The consolidated public sector budget nearly achieved balance, with a deficit equivalent to just under 1 percent of GDP. The current account surplus leaped to $7.96 billion while the overall balance of payments was $2.2 billion in the black.

Officials proclaimed these results as evidence that the economic program was working, but a closer look at the numbers showed that Venezuela was drifting away from the program. The improvement in the government's accounts was largely illusory; were it not for the $4 billion fourth-quarter oil windfall, the public might have registered a deficit equivalent to 8 percent of GDP. Monetary policy was excessively expansionary during the final five months of the year. Money supply (M2) increased at an 85 percent annual rate during this period, fueling renewed inflationary pressures which raised prices above the forecast (of less than 30 percent) for 1990. To make matters worse, the administration lost control of the budget process and ultimately accepted a hodgepodge drawn up by party leaders and enemies of reform that entailed deficits approaching 6–8 percent of GDP in 1991. Real interest rates became sharply negative and the bolivar became increasingly overvalued. The more sobering truths were downplayed because oil revenues made some of the numbers look good. But, as the bolivar became more overvalued, local producers started losing competitiveness and sales and crucial investment plans were deferred or canceled.

February 1991: A Second Chance

In December 1990, it appeared that the previous two years' efforts had been for naught, that the Pérez administration would repeat the pattern of its two immediate predecessors, both of which attempted modest reforms in their first two years only to revert to traditional policies for the remainder of their terms. Then war broke out in January. Oil prices plummeted once it became clear that supplies would not be disrupted, and Venezuela was jolted back to its senses. Fortunately, few resources had actually been committed to the grandiose spending plans drawn up in the heady months immediately preceding the plunge. The nation was given a second chance to reform.

To a remarkable extent, the administration—and the nation—appear to have taken advantage of that second opportunity. In the first nine months of 1991:

▲ The privatization program got off the ground, with the sale of three banks and Venezuela's international airline. The schedule for the fourth quarter included the telephone company, seven hotels, six sugar mills, and a shipyard, among others. Meanwhile, Sidor, the state steel mill, announced it would sell its partially constructed pipe mill to private investors. Public support for privatization is growing.

▲ A tax law was passed that reduced the top income bracket from 50 to 30 percent while reducing exceptions and loopholes for corporations; most personal exemptions were retained, however, and discussion of a value-added tax was postponed.

▲ Ports are being reorganized. Excess workers have been dismissed and featherbedding reduced. Responsibility for the ports is being transferred from the central government to the states.

▲ Trade liberalization was accelerated; the maximum tariff was reduced to 20 percent in February 1992, fourteen months ahead of schedule. At the same time, all tariff and nontariff barriers to trade with Colombia and other Andean Pact countries will be eliminated. Special tariff protection for "sensitive" items—of which only three remain—will be phased out by June 1992.

While the Perez government takes care of these matters, the principal opposition party, the social Christian Copei party, is redefining its doctrine, drawing heavily on Ludwig Erhard's "social market system."

The economy has reacted favorably. GDP increased 9.2 percent in 1991, the fastest annual rate in 28 years. Nonoil GDP was up 8.7 percent. Unemployment fell 1.1 percent, to 8.8 percent. More important, the average Venezuelan finally enjoyed a significant increase in personal income: nonoil GDP per capita increased 5.7 percent in 1991. Although still a long way from recovering the 11.8 percent loss in per capita income of 1989, Venezuelans were at long last beginning to reap some benefits from their sacrifices. Opinion polls published in October 1991 revealed that 57 percent of Venezuelans thought their personal situation was good, and 45 percent felt their situation would improve in the near term. These were the most positive readings recorded by pollsters in more than ten years.

Not all developments have been positive, however. Despite efforts to curb spending, the public sector deficit has not been brought under control; consequently, inflation remains high by Venezuelan standards. CTV labor leaders have succeeded in torpedoing proposed labor law reforms while blocking reorganization efforts in many areas. Health, education, and other public services have not improved. Corruption is rampant at most levels of government and efforts to reform the judiciary appear to be stalled. Similarly, reorganization of Venezuela's corrupt and inefficient customs service has gone nowhere. Far from attempting to enlist popular support to eliminate crooked practices, the parties are maneuvering intensely in an effort to prevent the electoral system from being opened further.

Despite these setbacks and uncertainties, there are many reasons for suggesting that President Pérez—and Venezuela—will stick with the reform campaign:

▲ Venezuela now has role models it can relate to. When the transition to a more open economy was first proposed, the only examples were Chile, a dictatorship, or Southeast Asia's four "tigers," whose cultures are completely different from Venezuela's. The situation is different today, since Venezuela can look toward Spain or Mexico for proof that reforms are beneficial if carried out properly, and toward Peru to see the disastrous consequences of pursuing populist policies.

▲ International sources of capital have conditioned their support and technical assistance on the opening up of Venezuela's economy. This support will be vital now that oil prices have fallen back to more normal levels. Though superficially strong, Venezuela's international position is in fact fragile. The country does not have sufficient international reserves, borrowing capacity, or oil revenues to finance a sustained growth-through-government-spending strategy.

▲ Social pressures are increasing. The public is demanding better public services, a more participatory electoral system, and clean government.

▲ More and more Venezuelans are beginning to understand the reasons for reform. With each passing day, it becomes harder to conceive of a reversal. Most businessmen, for instance, would not stand for a return to exchange controls. Nor would most accept renewed price controls.

Because the course of reform is bound to be unpredictable and to confuse people, it will not always be clear which way the momentum is going. The intense battle over severance benefit reforms illustrates these ambiguities. Since 1935, most departing employees have been entitled to receive a lump-sum payment equivalent to one month's pay for each year of service, based on the employee's monthly wage at the time of termination. This system has discouraged worker training and long-term employer-worker relationships while producing high turnover rates. In 1989, a small group of Venezuelan businessmen proposed replacing the traditional severance formula with a more modern benefit and pension program modeled after Chile's. The proposed system eliminates the bias against long-term employment, requiring that severance benefits be settled every three years, with the bulk of payments deposited in a pension fund controlled by the worker, not the employer. The administration supported the proposed changes, but labor stalwarts opposed them.

Several times over the past year, it appeared that the administration or the business sector had dropped the ball in the effort to modify severance benefits. But at other times it appeared that the contest had been won and that the Congress would approve a significant structural change for the first time in memory. But the legislature adjourned in August without taking up the bill. The administration has since reformulated the proposal for resubmission to the Congress. The outcome of the severance benefit debate will be a watershed event indicating which way the cause of reform is headed. In the end, strong leadership and public opinion will decide the issue.

Another upcoming event will also have a profound impact on the shape of things to come: the fate of the administration's value-added tax proposal. Perez's plan would broaden the government's revenue base while shifting the tax burden away from production and investment and onto consumption. A VAT would also ensure that the broadest number possible of Venezuelan consumers would bear their share of the cost of government. At the same time, the administration would be able to eliminate dozens of presently existing, low-yielding nuisance taxes. The VAT is widely opposed by politicians from all the major parties, mostly on demagogic or populist grounds. Yet without broad-ranging fiscal reform, there is little possibility that efforts to reorganize the public sector will go far.

Other issues that will indicate which way the wind is blowing include the privatization effort; the administration's willingness to continue adjusting the prices it charges for goods and services to reflect production or opportunity costs, including such politically sensitive items as gasoline; pending legislation concerning industrial property and patent protection law; and political and judicial reform.

The public sector deficit will be the most telling indicator of the program's direction. Eliminating the deficit is the macroeconomic program's most important pillar. The deficit was reduced in 1989 from around 10 percent of GDP to less than 2 percent. But that improvement was due to factors beyond the administration's control, and it did not last long. The challenge is to contain the deficit in 1991 and beyond, which can be accomplished only if the public sector is restructured. By one estimate, nonoil state company deficits will represent 5 percent of GDP in 1991. If these companies are revamped or privatized, the deficit will disappear.

Foreign investment used to be a sensitive issue in Venezuela. It now appears that foreign investment, yielding access to new markets and technology, will be welcomed, even in areas previously reserved for the state. Petróleos de Venezuela has invited foreign firms to participate in its ambitious investment program to raise capacity and diversify its product line. Inward investment will be boosted by reform, creating jobs and growth. More important, these investments in relatively unprotected industries will increase international competitiveness and give business and labor a greater stake in maintaining an outwardly oriented economy. With these successes, support for the program will grow, making it easier for the administration to implant additional reforms. A virtuous, self-reinforcing cycle is triggered.

Today it appears that President Pérez will resist pressures to modify or abandon his structural adjustment program. Staying on course is critically important because time is needed to build popular support for the changes and it will not be until 1992–93 that the benefits of the economic adjustment process begin to be realized. Recent experience of such other Latin American countries as Argentina or Brazil suggests strongly that "on again, off again" adjustment programs only deepen the economic crisis and generate public cynicism.

Even if Pérez stays with his program, serious obstacles will remain. One is the challenge of reorganizing such key economic institutions as the Finance Ministry or the Central Bank sufficiently to implement the new policies. Political and bureaucratic resistance is strong, and stalling tactics are likely to delay much-needed basic reforms.

There is no guarantee that Pérez's successor will share his commitment to a market economy. Pérez continues to battle with leaders of his own party over economic policy, and his power may erode as Venezuela moves toward local elections in 1992. The forthcoming political campaigns could once again be characterized by populist rhetoric and calls from all sides for a return to the old economic model. In a disturbing way, this scenario is already being enacted. The junior officers responsible for the February 1992 coup attempt used the political and economic situation as an excuse for their actions.

Grounds for optimism about Venezuela's future reside in the great progress that the administration expects will have been made by 1993 towards restructuring the economy. More important, perhaps, is that monetary resources, particularly another oil bonanza, are not likely to be available to finance a return to the old ways. Whoever is elected president in 1993 will continue to face unpopular political, economic, and social choices. If the market oriented economic reform program is sustained and nurtured, and if Venezuela's political institutions can adapt to permit greater political participation and openness, then the country faces a bright future. If not, the country will continue to stagnate economically. Oil wealth may continue to ease the process of economic deterioration and political decay, but it will not suffice to reverse it and, in fact, it may do more harm than good if it postpones the day of reckoning.

Venezuela: Economic Statistics

	1986	1987	1988	1989	1990	1991e
Domestic Economy (1984 bolivars, millions)						
Real GDP	448,285	464,341	491,372	449,262	473,031	516,468
% change	6.5	3.6	5.8	-8.6	5.3	9.2
Nonoil GDP	346,586	365,862	386,757	350,268	363,247	394,727
% change	6.0	5.6	5.7	-9.4	3.7	8.7
Oil GDP	86,150	86,945	93,924	93,561	106,275	116,829
% change	8.0	0.9	8.0	-0.4	13.6	9.9
GDP not allocated to any sector	15,549	11,534	10,691	5,433	3,509	4,913
% change	8.9	-25.8	-7.3	-49.2	-35.4	40.0
Per capita nonoil GDP	19,363	19,896	20,483	18,079	18,239	19,279
% change	3.2	2.8	3.0	-11.7	0.9	5.7
Inflation (% change)	12.70	40.30	35.50	81.00	36.50	31.00
Population (millions)	17.90	18.3	18.88	19.37	19.92	20.47
Unemployment (% of labor force)	10.30	8.50	6.90	9.60	9.90	8.80
Public sector borrowing (% of GDP)	4.4	4.6	-9.4	-1.4	1.0	0.5

e estimate
Sources: BCV, OCEI, Cordiplan, and VenEconomy estimates

	1986	1987	1988	1989	1990	1991e
External Economy (US$, millions)						
Exchange rate (bolivar-US$)						
Open market rate (year end)	23.55	30.50	39.30	43.10	50.75	61.63
Average rate for imports	9.42	12.48	14.83	38.50	48.75	52.92
Oil exports	7,592	8,927	8,023	9,862	13,780	12,233
Nonoil exports	1,530	1,510	2,059	3,053	3,498	2,894
Total exports	9,122	10,437	10,082	12,915	17,278	15,127
Imports	7,862	8,870	12,080	7,283	6,543	10,181
Trade balance	1,260	1,567	-1,998	5,632	10,735	4,946
Current account balance	-1,471	-1,390	-5,809	2,161	7,960	1,055
International reserves (year end; excludes PDVSA)	12,008	10,742	5,847	5,913	8,112	10,691

e estimate
Sources: BCV, OCEI, Cordiplan, and VenEconomy estimates

	1986	1987	1988	1989	1990	1991e
External Debt (US$, millions)						
Total external debt	33,274	32,991	34,739	32,486	31,938	30,561
% of GDP	54.7	70.4	57.7	80.6	66.2	67.5
% of exports goods, services & income	295.7	256.1	273.4	208.1	153.1	164.5
Total debt service	5,781	5,407	5,279	4,778	4,658	4,761
% of exports, goods, services & income	51.4	42.0	41.5	30.6	22.2	25.6

e estimate
Source: The Institute of International Finance

5 / Beyond Stabilization and Reform: The Argentine Economy in the 1990s

Roberto Bouzas

The Argentine economy has changed profoundly over the last decade. Economic institutions have been transformed to such a degree that they now bear little resemblance to those that dominated during most of the postwar period. Considerable progress has been made in restoring macroeconomic balances distorted by years of fiscal mismanagement, extensive borrowing from abroad, and large external shocks in the early 1980s. At the same time, a far-reaching process of structural reform has taken place, altering a number of crucial economic parameters and institutions. Interestingly enough, this transformation has followed a successful transition from authoritarian to democratic rule, and has been carried forward within a competitive and open political environment.

However, stability is still precarious, and sustained economic growth is far from restored. Furthermore, the reform process has entailed large economic and social costs. Overall, the economic record of Argentina in the 1980s was dismal: per capita GDP and real wages fell by almost a quarter and domestic investment rates almost halved. By the turn of the decade, net domestic capital formation was negative, and capital flight became recurrent as the nation suffered through two bouts of hyperinflation.

The author gratefully acknowledges the able research assistance of Juan Carlos Barboza and Saul Keifman.

In this context, policy instruments were rendered increasingly ineffective, and ultimately the very ability of the state to design and implement economic policies was called into question.

Most determinants of Argentina's economic performance in the last decade were domestic, and the country's economic prospects in the 1990s depend heavily on domestic initiatives. However, external factors will continue to play a critical role, shaping the environment within which domestic policies are carried forward. A more adequate treatment of the debt problem and the maintenance of open international markets (including the removal of distortions in agricultural trade) would certainly make a contribution to consolidating stability and facilitating economic growth. Equally important, forging a more sophisticated consensus on stabilization and reform policies (one that gives adequate consideration to their complexities and to competing demands) could ensure that the policies put in place will be carried out and will help ensure that Argentina does not squander its recent achievements. The importance of this latter factor cannot be overemphasized given the continued role of external actors (particularly international financial organizations) in influencing policy design and implementation.

The Economic Environment of the Democratic Transition

Postwar Argentina usually has been presented as a paradigm of an inward-oriented and overregulated economy. Until the mid-1970s, import substitution industrialization (ISI) delivered moderate rates of economic growth behind high tariff walls, though at the cost of mounting macroeconomic instability and disequilibria in public sector finances, resource allocation, and income distribution. Gradually, the public sector became overburdened by a myriad of spending demands within the context of a nonaccommodating tax base. In turn, scarce resources were usually allocated with little regard to social benefits and costs. Furthermore, the antitrade bias and heavy investment in capital-intensive industries distorted income distribution in favor of capital employed in production for the domestic markets. Recurrent balance of payments crises and the inflationary upsurge of 1975 underlined the limits of the prevailing development strategy. A poorly designed and implemented liberalization attempt in the late 1970s aggravated the problems created by the ISI strategy and served to highlight some of its most negative features.

An analysis of the heritage of ISI is beyond the scope of this paper. However, three developments since 1975 provide clues to understanding the dismal economic performance of Argentina in the past decade.[1] First, the consolidation of a "high-inflation regime" (a state of affairs characterized not just by the persistence of high inflation rates, but by certain formal and informal institutional arrangements adopted to accommodate private sector responses to uncertainty and macroeconomic instability) helped create a more volatile economic climate focused on short-term gains.

Second, the collapse in 1980 of the fragile Argentine financial system developed after World War II brought about a marked contraction in domestic financial intermediation and stimulated an extensive "dollarization" of private sector portfolios. As a result, remaining domestic financial intermediation was carried forward on a very short-term basis, involving, for the most part, financing disorganized public sector accounts at ever-increasing real interest rates.

Third, rapid debt accumulation in the late 1970s radically altered the structure of the country's payments balance, with factor payments (debt service) becoming a major determinant of current account deficits. High external indebtedness also rendered the economy very vulnerable to exogenous shocks such as increases in international interest rates, changes in the terms of trade, or the rationing of credit in world capital markets.

Just that kind of shock was in the making in 1982, when Mexico suspended payments on its debt. Although Argentina's balance of payments difficulties preceded the Mexican moratorium (private external liabilities were implicitly rescheduled in 1981, and the Falklands/Malvinas war brought about a de facto moratorium), the real troubles began after the Mexican episode barred most developing countries from international capital markets. The need to adjust to the cutoff of fresh lending precipitated hasty and inconsistent policy responses, which further increased capital flight, inflation rates, and fiscal disequilibria. In particular, the public sector's assumption (through subsidies) of private sector external liabilities worsened the already precarious position of the public sector accounts. As a result, the external problems posed by the debt crisis were compounded by its domestic—that is, fiscal—implications.

Thus, the transition from authoritarian to democratic rule took place in a particularly adverse economic context, appropriately characterized as one of "chaotic adjustment."[2] Between 1981 and 1983, per capita GDP contracted by almost 15 percent, the share of fixed investment in GDP fell from more than 19 percent to below 15 percent, and inflation rates accelerated furiously, recording monthly rates of about 15 percent by 1983. Similarly, in that year the budget deficit as a share of GDP was higher than 15 percent—an almost unprecedented level—and the monetization coefficient (M2/GDP) fell to about half the level recorded two years earlier. There were record debt service payments to cope with as well. By the end of 1983, the interest payment/export ratio had risen to about 70 percent, while the debt/GDP ratio had climbed beyond 50 percent.

Economic Stabilization and Reform in an Overindebted Economy

The elected government that took office in late 1983 faced a threefold economic challenge: to reduce macroeconomic imbalances and promote stabilization, to remove long-standing structural inefficiencies, and to restore external solvency. The political muscle to carry forward these far-reaching reforms was, however, weak. The Radical party of Raúl Alfonsín won the 1983 elections on the basis of a rhetoric emphasizing civil and political rights, with no clear-cut proposal for economic reform. The principal opposition, the Peronists, though unexpectedly defeated at the polls, remained strong.

Therefore, during its first year in office the new administration dealt with each of these distinctive—though interrelated—economic challenges with a "business-as-usual" approach. Since the fight against inflation did not include any major effort at fiscal consolidation, it left untouched one of the main sources of macroeconomic instability. In fact, reliance upon "gradualist" income policies and passive monetary management proved wholly insufficient. Instead of structural reform, the new government pursued a redistributive strategy based on the expectation of resumed economic growth fueled by the expansion of domestic demand. The foreign debt crisis could be solved by a more assertive stance vis-à-vis foreign creditors; candidly, Alfonsín's administration seemed to think that, as a newborn democracy, Argentina would qualify for special and more flexible treatment on the part of creditors.

Initially, this approach had a favorable impact on economic growth, public sector balances, and real wages, though at the cost of accelerating inflation and an appreciating domestic currency. In less than a year, the inconsistencies of economic policy had backfired; as a result, the administration was left with no option but to enforce a strict stabilization program under the auspices of the International Monetary Fund (IMF). Following a failure to comply with the terms of the IMF standby agreement, the minister of the economy resigned in early 1985.

The new economic team brought about a change in policy focus. The Austral plan launched in June 1985 became the first comprehensive attempt to control rampant price inflation, restore basic macroeconomic balances (particularly in the fiscal realm), and address the debt issue. Admittedly, with some delay and partly as a result of multilateral financial organizations' conditionality, after 1987 the Radical administration placed a new emphasis on structural reform. Its ability to deliver, however, was limited by strong congressional opposition, strengthened by the Peronist success in the 1987 parliamentary and local elections.

The Quest for Economic Stabilization

After 1985, the Radical administration regarded the reduction of macroeconomic imbalances and the promotion of a relatively stable economic environment as necessary—albeit not sufficient—conditions to restore economic growth. However, after some initial success with the Austral plan, a mix of design problems (fiscal restraint was too timid), external shocks (terms of trade moved against Argentine exports), and political and economic pressures (resistance to the erosion of workers' real earnings and a rapid return to wage indexation) reignited inflation and brought about the collapse of the stabilization attempt. Following the demise of the Austral plan in 1986, the government launched a series of ephemeral "stabilization packages" in an increasingly adverse political environment. Nothing worked. The radical party's candidate, Eduardo Angeloz, was defeated in the 1989 presidential race by Carlos Saul Menem of the Justicialista (Peronist) party. A hyperinflationary surge followed close upon the defeat of the Radical candidate.

Given their record, the Peronists' ascendancy sent a shudder through the financial markets. However, the first hyperinflationary episode of mid-1989 reinforced the priority assigned to economic stabilization by the newly elected Menem administration. It also rendered many policy instruments ineffective, sharply limiting the available options. In contrast to expectations, the Peronists deepened stabilization and structural reform policies and attempted to reestablish working relations with multilateral financial institutions as a prelude to a debt reduction agreement. As a result, for the past two years Argentina has followed a policy course closely associated with the recommendations of the so-called Washington consensus.[3] Three different "economic packages" were tried out in this period.[4] In between, a second hyperinflationary surge in January/February 1990 proved that uncertainty and instability still prevailed as two major features of the economic landscape (see Figure 1).

Notwithstanding their different theoretical underpinnings,[5] most recent attempts at economic stabilization have followed a similar path: an initial "policy shock" leads to a fall in inflation, a temporary improvement in fiscal balances, and lower real interest rates. After a few months, creeping inflation, progressive deterioration of public finances, and mounting real interest rates build up pressures that eventually force a crisis of confidence in the currency.

Although labor opposition to lower real wages and business resistance to the removal of subsidies have certainly complicated matters, the disappointing economic results of the late 1980s can be traced to three more fundamental reasons. First, the extent of the fiscal crisis was deeply aggravated by high external indebtedness (which in turn created an "internal transfer problem" stemming from the fact that, in contrast to Mexico, Chile, or Venezuela, the Argentine public sector did not generate foreign exchange that might be used to service the external debt), and the disarray of the tax collection system. Second, the absence of buffer mechanisms to compensate for unanticipated external shocks has encouraged speculative runs that have placed the domestic currency under pressure, leading to the collapse of otherwise reasonable stabilization attempts.[6] Finally, the prevailing policy consensus has had major weak spots and inconsistencies that increased the costs of stabilization and reform and, at times, even conspired against policy sustainability. Excessive concentration on short-run performance criteria on the part of multilateral financial institutions (particularly the IMF) has placed additional pressure on Argentina. Overlapping priorities have also frequently conspired against the consistency of policies; for example, the need to improve fiscal balances conflicted with attempts to reduce the anti-export bias of the trade regime by lowering tariffs and export taxes, and attempts to bring about a real devaluation of the currency for the sake of competitiveness raised inflationary pressures and increased external debt service. This tension between the complexities and competing demands of stabilization on the one hand and structural reform on the other continues to pose a challenge for Argentine policymakers.

Structural Reform since 1985

Structural reform covers three broad policy areas: the trade and payments system, the public sector, and the regulatory framework. Structural reform became the dominant priority of the economic agenda starting after 1987, about four years into Alfonsín's tenure, and it has always been the chief objective of the Menem administration. As a result, the institutional environment of the Argentine economy in the early 1990s is radically different from that which prevailed at the beginning of the democratic transition (see Figure 2).

Trade and payments reform. Postwar Argentina has displayed a strong inward orientation and a marked anti-export bias.[7] The main policy instruments have been protection of domestic production (by means of both tariff and nontariff barriers), taxation of traditional exports, and an overvalued exchange rate, which favored producers for the domestic market over exporters. After 1985, a number of steps were taken to remake this set of incentives. Whereas the trade regime has undergone a remarkable reform, exchange rate policies—notwithstanding the shift away from foreign exchange controls—have varied widely.

Trade policy since 1985 has reduced the level of protection conferred on domestic producers by removing nontariff barriers and lowering nominal tariffs.[8] In the mid-1980s, a large number of imports were subject to quantitative restrictions such as "prior consultation" requirements or outright prohibition. According to World Bank estimates, by early 1987 approximately 62 percent of total domestic manufacturing production was still protected by quantitative restrictions. In contrast, by early 1991 all quantitative restrictions had been lifted except those affecting the automobile sector.

Similarly, nominal tariff rates fell considerably throughout the period. Although on several occasions nominal tariffs were raised or special surcharges imposed in order to raise revenue for a resource-deprived public sector, there was widespread agreement that this was not sound policy. In the mid-1980s, the nominal tariff schedule (excluding a 15 percent temporary surcharge imposed by the Austral plan) varied between a minimum of zero percent and a maximum of 38 percent, with a production-weighted average rate of 28 percent. Special regimes for automobile and electronic industries conferred even higher nominal protection to these sectors. In contrast, by 1991 nominal tariffs had fallen to 35 percent (for automobiles and electronic products), with the rest of imports subject to a three-tiered schedule (5, 13, and 22 percent).

Figure 1
Stabilization Programs, 1985–91

	Incomes policy	Exchange rate policy	Monetary policy	Fiscal policy
"Austral plan" (June 1985)	Wage and price freeze. Conversion scale for existing contracts.	Foreign exchange control. Fixed exchange rate first and crawling-peg afterward.	Active in the beginning and passive afterward.	Restrictive fiscal policy. Emergency measures to increase revenue.
"Australito" (February 1987)	Wage and price freeze.	Foreign exchange control. Fixed exchange rate first and crawling-peg afterward.	No change.	No change.
October 1987	Wage and price freeze.	Free foreign exchange market for financial transactions. Controlled foreign exchange market for commercial transactions.	Financial markets' regulations are eliminated.	Tax-raising package submitted to Congress.

"Primavera plan" (August 1988)	Agreement to progressively reduce private and public sector prices.	Multiple exchange rates for commercial transactions. Free foreign exchange market for financial transactions.	Active. Main policy instrument of the plan.	No fiscal package (national elections upcoming).
"BB plan" (July 1989)	Price agreements with the private sector.	Foreign exchange control. Fixed exchange rate.	Passive.	Expenditure reduction.
"Bonex plan" (December 1989)	None.	Free foreign exchange market. Managed floating.	Very restrictive. Compulsory exchange of public domestic debt, including all term deposits for ten-year, dollar-denominated bonds.	Very restrictive, especially on expenditure side. Successive expenditure-reducing packages.
"Convertibility plan" (April 1991)	Initially, price agreements with the private sector. Indexation prohibited.	Free foreign exchange market. Fixed exchange rate with full convertibility.	Monetary creation limited by increase in international reserves.	Very restrictive. Tax-raising package submitted to Congress.

Figure 2
Major Structural Reforms, Mid-1980s through Early 1990s

Situation in Mid-1980s	Situation in Early 1990s
TRADE AND EXCHANGE RATE REGIME	
Foreign exchange controls.	Free foreign exchange market. As of April 1991, full convertibility.
High nominal tariffs and large dispersion of tariff rates.	Three tariff rates (5, 13, and 22 percent). Special 35 percent rate for automobiles and electronics.
Prohibitions and quantitative restrictions on imports.	Most quantitative restrictions eliminated.
PUBLIC SECTOR	
Large total and primary budget deficits.	Balanced budget and primary surplus in 1991.
Public sector expenditures equal large share of GDP.	Lower public sector expenditures (by 10 points of GDP).
Regressive tax structure. High evasion. Inefficient enforcement of tax collection.	Same. Administration's reform proposal under congressional consideration.
Three hundred public firms in monopoly or oligopolistic position in goods and service markets.	Large program of public sector divestiture on course.
REGULATION	
Controlled prices and wages.	Market-determined prices, initially with sectoral agreements. Collective negotiation for private sector wages. Public sector wages frozen. Indexation prohibited.
Controlled interest rates. Control of credit allocation. Large public financial sector.	Market-determined interest rates. Free allocation of credit by private banks. Shrinkage of public financial sector.
Control of international capital movements.	Free international capital movements.
Labor Contract Law suspended in 1976. Extensive government intervention in labor markets.	Labor Contract Law revived. Proposal submitted to Congress to make labor market more flexible.
Extensive regulation in goods markets.	Wide-ranging deregulation in goods and service markets, including oil production and distribution, agricultural production and trade, and foreign trade.

Generally, export policies have also shifted toward removing the antitrade bias characteristic of the postwar trade regime. Whereas in the mid-1980s maximum export taxes were 25 percent, by 1991 they had been largely eliminated, except for those on oilseeds and leather. However, as in the case of nominal tariffs, the extent and sustainability of export tax reduction depended on the urgency of fiscal needs. Just as important, Argentina's ability to offer incentives toward nontraditional exports has been seriously limited by its straitened finances.

In contrast to the protrade orientation of export and import policies, exchange rate policies have been inconsistent. In spite of widespread acceptance of the principle that preventing overvaluation was necessary to keep Argentine exports competitive, the currency has gone through periods of substantial appreciation, especially since 1988 (see Figure 3). Furthermore, the real exchange rate has been extremely volatile, breeding uncertainty and discouraging export-oriented investment and production. Periods of sustained real appreciation can be partly explained on two grounds: its short-run positive effect on inflation and price expectations, and its favorable impact on public sector finances. (The public sector has a deficit in its net foreign exchange balance.[9])

**Figure 3
Real Exchange Rate, 1983–91**

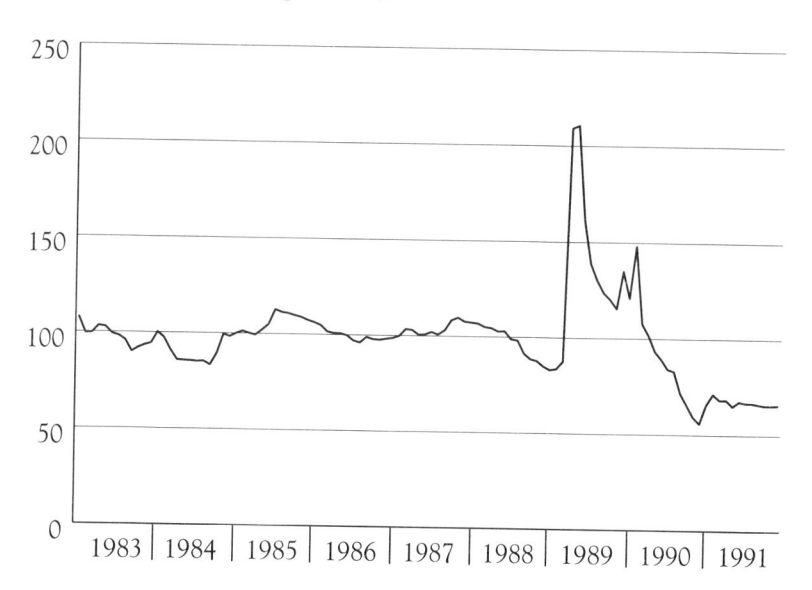

Exchange rate policy in the late 1980s did, however, show a consistent movement away from foreign exchange controls for current as well as for capital transactions.

Notwithstanding the shared perspective that inward orientation was no longer appropriate to foster economic growth, the initiatives undertaken to reintegrate Argentina into the world trading and financial system have varied significantly. In fact, the so-called export-oriented trade liberalization of 1986–87 (which combined moderate nominal tariff rates, incentives to nontraditional exports, and a high real exchange rate) was much different from the trade policy component of the 1991 Convertibility plan, which brought together low nominal tariff rates and an appreciating real exchange rate. Different approaches toward subregional economic integration were also clear: although the program of mutual trade liberalization with Brazil launched in 1985 (later joined by Paraguay and Uruguay with the goal of creating a Common Market, MERCOSUR, by 1995) has remained a priority, it has been largely subject to changing trade policies. The 1985–86 emphasis on sectoral preferential liberalization and the promotion of intraindustry trade was progressively replaced by across-the-board tariff cuts in a context of unilateral trade liberalization.

Public sector reform. The public sector reform occupied center stage in Argentine economic policymaking in the 1980s. This was partly the result of the pervasive effects of large fiscal imbalances, which were compounded by the debt crisis and further fed by two hyperinflationary surges. Public sector reform was implemented with varying degrees of success in three main areas: promotion of fiscal equilibrium, change in the composition of public sector revenues and expenditures, and privatization of public firms.

The degree of fiscal adjustment that took place in the Argentine economy during the 1980s is impressive. From an average of 14.5 percent of GDP in the 1981–83 crisis period, the deficit fell to just 2.1 percent of GDP in 1990 and to zero in 1991.[10] Net of interest payments, primary budget deficits also shrank markedly from 11.65 percent of GDP in 1983 to a 2.5 percent surplus in 1991. However, this process has not been smooth, and occasionally—particularly in periods of accelerating inflation or hyperinflation—disequilibrium increased markedly.

Deficit reduction has been primarily the result of lower real expenditures, which decreased by 10 percent of GDP between 1983 and 1990.[11] In relative terms, this reduction has fallen most heavily upon capital expenditures, whose share of GDP was almost halved in the period. In absolute terms, however, current expenditures have contracted more (about 7 points of GDP). Although the decline affected most expenditure categories, the composition of public expenditures has changed substantially. On the one hand, there was the steep drop-off of capital investment's share in total government expenditure and GDP. On the other, central government transfers (to the provinces and to retirement and pension systems) rose sharply in proportion to total government expenditure.

Overall, fiscal revenue as a share of GDP did not change much between 1983 and 1990, although there have been some changes in its composition, particularly a rise in capital revenues (that is, privatization proceeds), a reduction in the share of nontax current revenues, and a fall in direct taxes, which were, in any event, only minor contributors to total government revenues at the beginning of the period. Occasionally, government revenues have been given a temporary boost by "forced savings" programs or special mechanisms to expedite taxpayer compliance. There is, however, widespread agreement that the inability to improve upon tax collection was one of the most disappointing aspects of fiscal policy reform in Argentina in the 1980s. This failure draws attention to the need to rebuild public institutions, something too easily overlooked in the past and to which we turn later.

In recent years, Argentina has also undergone an extensive process of public sector divestiture. As of the mid-1980s, the state's productive activities were still extensive. According to one source, more than three hundred public firms were either monopolies (in energy, rail and air transportation, communications, sewage disposal, water provision, and arms production) or held dominant market positions (in the financial, petrochemical, maritime transportation, and steel sectors).[12] Although the shift in policy toward divestiture began in 1987, the political stalemate between the Alfonsín government and Congress meant that no genuine progress was recorded until after the elections of 1989.

In the two largest privatizations—and other comparatively minor ones—carried forward by the Menem administration, the government swapped equity in a telecommunications company and an international air carrier for a reduction of its external debt obligations, seeking the best deal creditors would offer in an effort to reduce the stock of external debt. In this manner, the Argentine debt conversion-cum-privatization program became the world's largest: in 1990 alone, the foreign debt was reduced by more than $7 billion via debt equity conversion.[13]

Two problems have recently slowed the initial impetus of public sector divestiture. The government's urgency to get the privatization process in gear (out of fiscal despair and the need to establish reform credentials) led it to transfer public firms to the private sector without having in place an appropriate regulatory framework. When the activity in question is a natural monopoly, as in the case of the telecommunications company, the implications are particularly serious. The same urgency has strengthened the bargaining stance of private bidders, who then seek to renegotiate the originally agreed-upon terms. This happened in the case of the international airline, and similar problems arose in the transfer of national highways and rail freight networks to the private sector.

Economists have raised caveats regarding the potential consequences of extensive privatization programs in a context of macroeconomic instability and great fiscal strain.[14] These are wholly applicable here, but the recent experience of Argentina raises new quandaries as well. Haphazard implementation of privatization programs can have long-lasting negative effects upon international competitiveness (such as high telecommunications tariffs relative to international standards) and public sector accounts (as in the case of payments made to compensate for changing originally poorly devised conditions in contracts). Furthermore, the short-run benefits to the balance of payments from privatization in which foreign investors participate through debt conversion schemes may be counterbalanced by profit remittances in the future, particularly if the activities in which foreign firms participate promise high monopoly rents.

Deregulation. The post-1985 period has also been one of active deregulation of markets for goods, services, and factors of production. Traditionally, Argentina has been a heavily regulated economy, with the state intervening directly or indirectly in its markets.[15] Regulations were particularly burdensome in financial and labor markets, as well as for certain specified goods. Furthermore, comprehensive regimes of price and wage controls were frequently implemented in the battle against inflation. In the late 1970s, one of the most perverse aspects of regulatory policy was the various industrial promotion schemes set up by the military regime, which severely burdened public sector accounts.

Throughout the postwar period, financial regulation was carried forward through various mechanisms like controlled interest rates, central bank allocation of credit, and compulsory lending to the public sector. Furthermore, large public financial institutions, which were responsible for about 50 percent of total deposits, exerted considerable market leverage. Liberalization was attempted in the late 1970s, with disastrous results: financial markets crashed in 1980 and domestic lending came to a virtual standstill. The proliferation of informal financial channels circumvented most regulations and gave rise to a new deregulatory wave—albeit more moderate than a decade earlier—in 1987, when control of interest rates was terminated and other restrictions on the operation of private financial institutions were phased out. More recently, financial deregulation advanced further as the activity of publicly owned financial institutions was severely restricted. November 1991 brought a sweeping deregulation package that included the elimination of most remaining restrictions affecting the operation of capital markets.

Argentine labor markets have also been subject to heavy regulation. The Labor Contract Law set *de minimis* working conditions, on which unions and workers' associations could improve by means of collective bargaining. This legislation has commonly been suspended for long periods, while the government took direct responsibility for the determination of wages and salaries. The failure of the Alfonsín government to reform legislation governing labor unions was followed by a period of large-scale labor unrest. In 1987, though, collective negotiations (suspended since 1976) were reestablished. Finally, in 1991 Carlos Menem proposed new legislation to promote flexibility in labor markets. This legislation authorizing short-term contracts and reducing overall labor costs is under congressional consideration.

Deregulation has also advanced in markets for goods (notably for prime agricultural products like cereals, sugar, tobacco, and meat) and services. Probably the outstanding example has been that of oil production and distribution, traditionally under the control of the state oil monopoly. Although the association of the state oil company with private firms for the purpose of carrying forward exploratory activities goes back to 1987, oil sector deregulation was adopted as policy by the Menem administration in late 1989, and took effect in 1991. The main changes were privatization of "secondary areas," state oil company joint ventures with private firms for the purpose of exploiting "primary areas," deregulation of oil and natural gas production and distribution (including foreign trade), and market determination of prices for all types of fuels.

Since the mid-1970s, various industrial promotion schemes have deeply influenced the establishment and allocation of industrial activities.[16] These regimes have been heavily criticized for their lack of transparency and audit, overlapping or conflicting priorities, and unassessed costs and benefits. Since industrial promotion consisted mostly of tax deferrals and exemptions, it represented a serious drain on the treasury as well as a massive transfer of scarce resources from the taxpayer to private firms. Most industrial promotion benefits were temporarily suspended in 1989, but they were restored once the period set by the Economic Emergency Law expired one year later, although enforcement became much stricter. (In the past, poor auditing meant that private firms were granted tax benefits irrespective of whether original targets were met or not.) More recently, the November 1991 deregulatory package ended several remaining sectoral benefits. However, there is uncertainty as to how many incentives will eventually survive. Improved supervision and enforcement of applicable regulations and more informed and objective assessment of costs and benefits would greatly contribute to reducing the fiscal burden of the remaining programs.

Restoration of External Solvency: An Unfinished Task

Since the early 1980s, Argentina has had one of the worst showings among the middle-income developing countries by any gauge of economic performance. One of the most disappointing outcomes of the decade was that, notwithstanding large adjustments undertaken throughout the period, critical indicators of the nation's basic solvency did not improve until very recently, and then for exogenous and/or accounting reasons. In fact, debt/export, debt/GDP, and interest/export ratios all remained at extremely high levels, reaching their peaks in 1987. More recently, they have improved under the favorable influence of falling interest rates in world capital markets and the debt reduction-cum-privatization program. Similarly, in spite of sizable transfers of capital abroad, external debt increased by almost 40 percent between 1983 and 1990.

The foreign debt crisis has been a constant source of macroeconomic uncertainty and instability as well as a permanent drain on resources. It required large trade surpluses to finance payments to creditors overseas. On average, between 1983 and 1990 resource transfers abroad amounted to about $3.4 billion a year, compared to inflows of approximately $900 million in the second half of the 1970s.

Considering that normalization of external financial relations has consistently ranked high among policy priorities, progress has been modest. Relations with multilateral financial institutions have generally been strained, and the comprehensive financial package agreed to with private creditors in 1987 turned out to be very short-lived.[17] In fact, since April 1988 Argentina has had a nondeclared partial moratorium on servicing its debt to private creditors. Relations with commercial banks have not deteriorated further only because of the attractiveness of the debt conversion-cum-privatization program launched in 1990, which has been received warmly at least by the largest creditors.

Argentina's external debt position does not look encouraging today. In the first place, even after the sharp fall in interest rates of the last couple of years, the indicators of solvency referred to earlier are still disappointing. In the second place, after more than two years of de facto moratorium, accumulated interest arrears amount to about $8 billion. The issue of how to deal with interest arrears will prove difficult to resolve with commercial banks, particularly if international reserves cannot be used to cancel interest arrears due to the legal restrictions imposed by the Convertibility Law.[18] Finally, until mid-1991, negotiations with international financial organizations were still on and off, notwithstanding clear progress toward reducing fiscal imbalances. More recently, Argentina has been capable of meeting the targets included in the last standby agreement with the IMF for two consecutive quarters, opening the door to a three-year extended facility loan.

More fundamentally, Argentina's debt problem is unlikely to be solved by any debt reduction agreement alone. The Brady plan and the debt component of the Enterprise for the Americas Initiative are steps forward, but they are clearly insufficient.[19] Previous experiences with debt reduction programs negotiated with commercial banks show that these agreements do not provide substantial relief for debtor countries. Similarly, relief as a result of cancellation, reduction, or sale of debts owed to U.S. official agencies will not get to the root causes of the problem. Unless favorable conditions (especially low interest rates) continue to prevail in international capital markets or a return of flight capital is achieved, in the next few years the shadow of the foreign debt crisis will continue to loom large over Argentina.

The Road Ahead: Beyond Stabilization and Reform in the 1990s

While government efforts at stabilization have posted a mixed record, economic reform measures have been sweeping and thorough. Yet a clear-cut movement toward outward orientation, less government intervention, and a larger role for the market has not led to resumed economic growth. Various reasons can be cited for this failure. First, design and implementation problems have limited policy effectiveness. Some of these are the result of political constraints. Others, however, are the consequence of an approach to stabilization and reform that did not give enough consideration to internal consistency and external shocks. In particular, the short-run conditionality demanded by the IMF has been poorly suited to the complexity created by attempts to achieve economic stabilization and reform simultaneously. On occasion, this has threatened policy sustainability and government credibility.

It may be simply that more time is needed before reforms lead to economic growth. However, there is an emerging intellectual consensus that given the conditions faced by most Latin American economies, even thoroughgoing economic reform might not be sufficient to restore growth. Although an enhanced role for market signals, less government intervention, and fewer distortions might all be necessary conditions, the question is whether they will, in and of themselves, restore basic incentives for investment, repatriation of capital, and sustained expansion.[20]

The debt burden will continue to exact a toll in terms of increased volatility and resource transfers out of the country. The opening up of the Argentine economy in a context of greater global interdependence can only heighten the nation's vulnerability to interest rate hikes.

While the prospects for resumed growth are uncertain in a climate where stabilization remains the paramount objective, the needs of the state and society at large for investment and expanded opportunity cannot be postponed indefinitely. Three issues that have been, under the pressure of events, relatively neglected in the recent past will merit closer attention in the future:

Facing increased poverty and inequality. Traditionally, Argentina has been a wealthy country by Latin American standards, a fact reflected in the generally favorable social and economic indicators in the areas of health, education, nutrition, and the extent of poverty. Following decades of slow economic growth or even stagnation, this long-standing distinction no longer prevails. In particular, the disappointing economic performance of the 1980s greatly aggravated already unfavorable postwar trends. As literacy, employment, and public health troubles increase, Argentina has become a much more inegalitarian society than ever before.

Throughout the 1980s, labor market conditions deteriorated markedly, as might be expected in such a poor economic climate.[21] A regressive shift occurred in income distribution: wage earners' share in total income fell markedly and income by family displayed a clear tendency toward concentration. The number of families below subsistence level grew.[22]

These worsening social and economic indicators have not received as much attention as they merit, probably as a result of the sense of impotence that prevails among both analysts and policymakers. Still, they are bound to become critical political issues if not effectively addressed in the future. Although no clear-cut relationship between economic perfomance and political regimes has been established, increased political participation at a time of shrinking economic opportunities may be an explosive combination for any government in office.[23] The situation will demand policies specifically designed to deal with the mounting problems of poverty and inequality. The reach and effectiveness of such policies will be heavily dependent upon the fiscal condition of the state as well as its capacity to design and properly implement them. However, the challenges of poverty and inequality will continue to mount unless economic growth can be restored.

Establishing a favorable climate for growth and investment. Low rates of growth have been a dominant characteristic of the Argentine economy since the mid-1970s, but economic performance in the 1980s was especially bad. There is a consensus that reform and adjustment policies may improve the structure of incentives, stimulate a better allocation of resources, and therefore contribute to future economic growth. It is unlikely, though, that the Argentine economy will be able to restore economic growth on a sustainable basis unless net capital formation recovers from the negative values recorded in recent years.

How to restore incentives for expansion of output and how to finance investment expenditures are the critical questions. There are strong indications that the overwhelming preoccupation with market signals and efficient resource allocation characteristic of the so-called Washington consensus may be only a part of the answer. Residual uncertainty in economies that have been exposed to prolonged periods of stagnation and macroeconomic instability (high inflation, financial volatility, and payment crises) may discourage capital inflows (or reflows) and investment in physical capital even if there is a successful stabilization.[24] This problem may be aggravated if the country remains overburdened with foreign debt, which keeps alive the possibility of a payments or inflationary crisis down the road.[25]

A reduction of the outflow of capital through debt reduction or cancellation would certainly make a positive contribution to increased savings and improved expectations. Similarly, progress in multilateral trade talks in the Uruguay Round of the GATT system (particularly on the vital subject of agriculture) would contribute to the well-being of Argentine producers. The prospects for sustained progress in freeing agricultural trade might also foster a resumption of capital accumulation.

Reconstructing the public sector. Reform and reconstruction of public institutions will be essential if Argentina is to take full advantage of its growth potential. Almost a decade ago, Carlos Diaz Alejandro referred to this issue when he argued that, in the contemporary Latin American setting, institutions seemed to be weaker the more public they were, the public sector being an extreme case.[26] In the early 1990s, it is interesting to note that those countries in which stabilization was relatively easier to achieve and in which the expectation of renewed economic growth was restored earlier were precisely those with comparatively moderate budgetary problems and public sector disarray.

In the case of Argentina, the 1980s were a period not only of economic decline but also of pervasive public sector crisis. The state overextended itself in the production and provision of services, contributing to a deep fiscal crisis. The morass of government obligations led to a dramatic reduction of its ability to design and carry forward policies in the areas where it was most needed. Even administrative routines have become confused, inhibiting efficient policymaking and follow-up. Two successive hyperinflationary episodes damaged the government's credibility and constricted further its policy options.

Public sector reconstruction will require financial balance. Since public expenditures have already contracted sharply in the last decade, the remedy for chronic deficits will have to be found in strengthened tax collection. This is as much a matter of administrative capacity as of political decisionmaking, which raises another critical issue of state reconstruction: the proper functioning of the civil service, including an efficient and working system of internal control and supervision.

It is difficult to envisage a resumption of sustained economic growth and a reversal of the growing incidence of poverty unless high priority is attached to the task of building up the capacity of the public sector to design and effectively implement reform policies. The common argument that Latin American countries characteristically displayed "too much state intervention" has missed the critical issue of the nature of the intervention itself. Neglect of public sector reform may have led to policy recommendations that further weakened a key agent of economic growth. Even under the most conservative scenario, public investment will have to grow rapidly in order to overcome the backlog of infrastructural needs left over from the austere heritage of the 1980s. More generally, given that public and private investment are complementary, a restoration of the catalytic role of the public sector may be a sine qua non for future prosperity.

Conclusions

The Argentina of the early 1990s is a very different place from Argentina in 1980: the economy is now quite open to foreign trade and capital movements, government expenditures have been reduced, and privatization and deregulation have progressed markedly. There remains, however, much uncertainty about whether Argentina is in fact stable and poised for an economic takeoff.

Most of the remaining challenges are domestic in nature. There can be no doubt that consolidating economic stabilization and reform, restoring creditworthiness abroad, alleviating poverty, clearing away obstacles to productivity and investment, and reconstructing the public sector will all demand continuing domestic initiatives. However, the external environment can make a decisive contribution to keeping the country on the right track. In an "age of diminished expectations,"[27] it does not seem likely that external actors—particularly the United States—will make costly commitments to ease the economic difficulties of Argentina. The agenda of U.S.-Argentine relations will be dominated mostly by global economic issues such as external debt, foreign trade, and investment flows, but within these parameters, useful discussions are still possible.

In the first place, although the debt crisis is not as threatening as it once was, it remains a major source of uncertainty and instability for many Latin American countries. The secondary place to which the debt crisis has slipped in the hemispheric agenda over the last couple of years has been more the result of favorable global developments (falling interest rates) and the events in Mexico (in turn favorably affected by the prospects of a free trade agreement with the United States and Canada) than of any fundamental improvement. External shocks could still disrupt the flow of repayments and fresh lending. The next time around, a large share of the impact will be felt by multilateral institutions rather than commercial banks, which have largely succeeded in reducing their exposure to Latin America.

Open access to external markets will remain critical to trade and investment flows. The Bush administration's proposal to negotiate free trade areas with Latin American countries offers the promise of more secure access to the U.S. market, although there is uncertainty as to how far it would go in changing the present composition of U.S. trade barriers. For Latin American countries, particularly in the Southern Cone, a working multilateral system is the best guarantor of the benefits of international trade. Therefore, successful completion of the Uruguay Round negotiations (including a substantive agreement in the area of agricultural production and trade) is a must.

The opportunity to benefit from a positive international environment will be proportional to the progress made in achieving stabilization and promoting more efficient and competitive economies at home. Success will require creative thinking and a willingness to try new approaches. The prevailing consensus on development, stabilization, and reform policies has been exposed as inadequate; a more sophisticated set of accords is needed at a time when the influence of external actors on policy design will remain significant. The oversimplified policy arguments of the 1980s may have generated easy-to-follow rules, but they can hardly provide appropriate recipes for action in the face of complex problems such as those posed by economic stabilization and structural reform. It would be a great loss if the political goodwill carefully built up by two successive democratic governments were eroded by obstinate approaches that lack, in the end, solid analytical foundations.

Notes

1. J. M. Fanelli and R. Frenkel, "Argentina's Medium-Term: Problems and Prospects," *Documentos CEDES* no. 28 (Buenos Aires: Centro de Estudios del Estado y la Sociedad [CEDES], 1989).

2. M. Damill and R. Frenkel, "Malos Tiempos: La Economia Argentina en la Decada de los Ochenta," mimeo, CEDES, Buenos Aires, 1990.

3. J. Williamson, "What Washington Means by Policy Reform," in *Latin American Adjustment: How Much has Happened?*, ed. J. Williamson (Washington, D.C.: Institute for International Economics, 1990).

4. The three major "economic packages" were the so-called BB plan of July 1989, the Bonex plan of December 1989, and the Convertibility plan of April 1991.

5. The theoretical basis of the successive stabilization attempts varied from the "heterodox" approach of the Austral plan (which emphasized the use of incomes policies and foreign exchange controls) to the free market orientation of the Convertibility plan. The policy environment into which the stabilization plans were launched also differed greatly.

6. The impact of the sharp fall in the terms of trade in 1986–87 (partly attributable to the "agricultural subsidies war" between the United States and the European Community) is a clear case in point.

7. The World Bank has characterized the Argentine economy in the postwar period as one of the most inward oriented; see World Bank, *World Bank Development Report* (Washington, D.C.: World Bank, 1987). For an analysis of Argentina's postwar trade regime, see J. Berlinski, "Trade Policies in Argentina (1964–1988)," mimeo, Instituto di Tella, Buenos Aires, 1989.

8. Berlinski, "Trade Policies in Argentina."

9. The public sector has to use domestic currency to buy foreign exchange to service external debts. Hence, a real appreciation implies that fewer pesos are required to buy the same amount of US$.

10. For a comprehensive analysis of public sector structure and reform in the post-1985 period, see Comision Economica para America Latina (CEPAL), "La Desarticulación del Pacto Fiscal. Una Interpretación sobre la Evolución del Sector Público Argentino en las dos Ultimas Decadas," working paper no. 36, CEPAL, Buenos Aires, 1990.

11. Expenditure and revenue figures are those of the central government.

12. Fundación de Investigaciones Económicos Latinoamericanas (FIEL), *Regulaciones y Estancamiento: El Caso Argentino* (Buenos Aires: Ediciones Manantial, 1988).

13. Between 1989 and 1991, the most significant privatizations included concessions granted to operate TV and radio stations; the transfer of the operation and maintenance of 10,000 km of national highways and more than 5000 km of railway freight networks; the sale of 60 percent of the telecommunications company (an additional 10 percent was allocated to employees); 85 percent of the international air carrier (an additional 5 percent was allocated to employees); the partial sale of petrochemical firms; and leases and public-private cooperative ventures to extract oil. Steps in the near future include, among others, sale of the remaining 30 percent of the telecommunications company and privatization of an additional 4500 km of national highways plus suburban rail systems, selected long-distance railways, and electricity and natural gas distribution systems.

14. P. Meller, "Chile," in Williamson, *Latin American Adjustment*.

15. For a comprehensive analysis of Argentina's regulatory framework, see FIEL, *Regulaciones y Estanciamento: El Caso Argentino*, 1988.

16. For a review of the main industrial promotion schemes since the mid-1970s, see B. Kosacoff and D. Aspiazu, *La Industria Argentina: Desarrollo y Cambios Estructurales* (Buenos Aires: Centro Editor de America Latina (CEAL)-CEPAL, 1988).

17. For an exhaustive analysis of the evolving relationship with private and official creditors in the 1980s, see R. Bouzas and S. Keifman, "Deuda Externa y Negociaciones Financieras en la Decada de los Ochenta: Una Evaluación de la Experiencia Argentina," *Serie de Documentos e Informes de Investigación* no. 98, Facultad Latinoamericana de Ciencias Sociales (FLACSO), Buenos Aires, October 1990.

18. The Convertibility Law is a key component of the Convertibility plan launched in April 1991. It established that the domestic monetary base has to be fully backed by international reserves.

19. For an assessment of the Brady plan's achievements so far, see R. Bouzas, "Las Relaciones Economicas entre Estados Unidos y los Paises de America Latina y el Caribe en 1990," *Serie de Documentos e Informes de Investigación* no. 114, FLACSO, Buenos Aires, June 1991. The

potential implications of the debt component of the Enterprise for the Americas Initiative are discussed in R. Feinberg, "Deuda, Comercio e Inversion en la Iniciativa para las Americas," *America Latina/Internacional* (Buenos Aires) 8, no. 28 (April/June 1991).

20. R. Dornbusch, "Policies to Move from Stabilization to Growth," *Proceedings of the World Bank Annual Conference on Development Economics* (Washington, D.C.: World Bank, 1990), and J. M. Fanelli, R. Frenkel, and G. Rozenwurcel, "Growth and Structural Reform in Latin America: Where We Stand," *Documentos CEDES* no. 57 (Buenos Aires: CEDES, 1990).

21. L. A. Beccaria, "Industrialización, Mercado de Trabajo y Distribuición del Ingreso," mimeo, CEPAL, Buenos Aires, 1989.

22. Instituto Nacional de Estadisticas y Censos (INDEC), "La Pobreza en el Conurbano Bonaerense," study series no. 13 (Buenos Aires: INDEC, 1989).

23. On the relationship between economic performance and political regimes, see, for example: R. Kaufman, "Industrial Change and Authoritarian Rule in Latin America: A Concrete Review of the Bureaucratic-Authoritarian Model," in *The New Authoritarianism in Latin America*, ed. D. Collier (Princeton, N.J.: Princeton University Press, 1979), and A. Hirschmann, "The Turn to Authoritarianism in Latin America and the Search for its Economic Determinants," in *Essays in Trespassing: Economics to Politics and Beyond*, ed. A. Hirschmann (Cambridge: Cambridge University Press, 1984).

24. Dornbusch, "Policies to Move From Stabilization to Growth."

25. Fanelli, Frenkel, and Rozenwurcel, "Growth and Structural Reform in Latin America."

26. C. Diaz Alejandro, "Latin American Debt: I Don't Think We Are in Kansas Anymore," *Brookings Papers on Economic Activity* 2 (Washington, D.C.: The Brookings Institution, 1984).

27. P. Krugman, *The Age of Diminished Expectations* (Cambridge, Mass.: MIT Press, 1990).

ARGENTINA: ECONOMIC STATISTICS

	1986	1987	1988	1989	1990	1991e
Domestic Economy						
Real GDP (% change)	5.6	2.2	-2.7	-4.4	0.4	4.5[1]
Per capita real GDP (% change)	4.4	1.0	-3.9	-5.6	-0.8	3.0[2]
Inflation (% change)	90.1	131.3	342.9	3,079.5	2,313.9	171.7
Real exchange rate[3]	100.0	103.0	98.3	133.1	90.1	67.1
Real wage rate[4]	100.6	92.5	89.1	69.2	77.9	72.8[3]
Population (millions)	31.04	31.50	31.97	32.45	32.94	na
Unemployment (% of labor force)	5.2	5.7	6.1	8.1	6.2	na
Budget deficit[5] (% of GDP)	-4.7	-4.4	-4.7	-6.2	-2.1	0.2
Primary budget deficit[5] (% of GDP)	-1.8	-0.5	-1.0	0.1	2.2	2.5

e estimate
[1] Economic Commission for Latin America (ECLA/CEPAL) estimate
[2] ECLA estimate
[3] First ten months annualized, index 1986 = 100
[4] Index 1983 = 100
[5] Nonfinancial public sector

Sources: Central Bank of the Argentine Republic (CBAR/CBRA)
The Institute of International Finance
Statistics and Census National Institute (SCNI/INDEC)

External Economy (US$, millions)

	1986	1987	1988	1989	1990	1991e[1]
Merchandise exports	6,852	6,360	9,134	9,573	12,354	5,716
Merchandise imports	-4,724	-5,820	-5,324	-4,199	-4,079	-3,032
Trade balance	2,128	540	3,810	5,374	8,275	2,684
Current account balance	-2,859	-4,238	-1,572	-1,305	1,789	-1,038
Total external debt	51,422	58,324	58,473	63,314	60,973	63,038
% of GDP	56	61	61	67	63	62
% of exports goods	750	917	640	661	494	551
Total debt service						
% of exports goods	63	65	51	63	47	46

e estimate
[1] First half of 1991
Sources: CBAR and ECLA

National Income, Savings and Investment (% of GDP)

	1986	1987	1988	1989	1990
GDP	100	100	100	100	100
National income	90.9	90.7	90.6	89.0	87.4
Consumption	84.0	83.4	80.5	80.3	77.5
National savings	6.8	7.3	10.1	8.7	9.9
External savings	4.6	5.8	2.0	0.0	-1.7
Investment	11.4	13.1	12.0	8.7	8.1
Trade balance	4.5	3.5	7.5	10.9	14.4

Source: Economic Commission for Latin America (ECLA/CEPAL)

6 / Mexico: Debt and Reform

Luis Rubio

Mexico is well on its way out of the debt crisis of the 1980s. In fact, debt has largely ceased to be a central economic policy issue.[1] Although total debt is still high, its economic importance is declining. As manufactured exports grow and the economy recovers, the importance of debt and debt servicing diminish relative to the size of the economy.[2] This is good news after almost a decade of stagnation and falling real incomes. The 1989 restructuring agreement with creditor banks, whereby the banks agreed to write off part of their Mexican assets, tells only a small part of the story. The real change in Mexico's outlook began in 1985 with profound economic reform.

More important than the shrinkage of debt in relative terms has been its decline in psychological weight—negative expectations about Mexico's future have been replaced by cautious optimism. This change in national outlook owes less to the debt agreement than to the transformation in Mexico's economy over the last seven years through economic policy. Until 1982, Mexico's economy was highly protected by tariff and nontariff barriers, government held a large equity stake in the economy, and competition was limited to the few sectors of the economy where monopolies or oligopolies did not predominate. A highly centralized and semiauthoritarian political system used special economic policy to maintain interests. This cozy world is collapsing, but an open and competitive economy and society has not yet fully replaced it.

The economic reform under way is gradually transforming Mexican society as well. As imports have poured in (increasing the import bill by more than $20 billion in the last four years), competition has become the driving force behind the economy. Many firms and sectors are thriving in the new environment while others fail. Whole industries—for example, toys and electronics—have been virtually wiped out. In other industries, however, entrepreneurship and technological skills have begun to create what may eventually become a solid basis for Mexico's development. This period of adjustment has entailed bankruptcies, unemployment, and shifts in the relative economic strength of regions as well as industries. How to complete and consolidate this extraordinary process of change remains the big political issue in Mexico today.

Economic change breeds political change. As regions, economic sectors, and firms begin to feel the effects of competition, new relationships are growing within firms, among businesspeople and politicians, between labor and government. Every economic change has significant political consequences. The context and rules of the economy are changing, impelling similar dramatic changes in the nature of the political system. A new Mexico is gradually emerging under the thrust of new political realities and the buildup of small but significant changes in the rules and structure of the political system. For example, these changes are being pushed by a government that has accepted the challenges posed by Mexico's backwardness and stagnation and the changes that have taken place in the rest of the world over the last decade and a half. Because reform began with a government initiative, not a popular movement, it has had to win support as it begins to bring about economic recovery. To be consolidated, reform has to work its way into every layer of society, developing a constituency not just for the reform government but for reform itself.

After decades of misgovernment, however, Mexicans are wary of any governmental policy. The government's initiative toward closer economic ties with the United States therefore has more than just economic significance. The search for a trade agreement was motivated by the desire to consolidate domestic economic reform, conclude the economic stabilization process, and set the stage for a transformation of the political system. Each element dovetails with the others as long as Mexicans believe that reform signifies a basic—and permanent—shift in priorities. The trade negotiations between Mexico and the United States thus have enormous political meaning for both nations, and their outcome will be crucial for consolidating Mexico's reform over the long term.

The success or failure of Mexico's transformation will have repercussions far beyond its borders. Reforming a society frozen in time entails not only liberalization and deregulation but also direct hits against traditional vested interests. The transition from a closed society and economy into a modern, responsible one implies changes in structures, habits, traditions, and political culture. Success in transforming its society and polity along these lines will mean that Mexico has the ability not only to participate in international markets but to become a modern democracy as well.

Mexico's reform still has to prove itself. At issue is a country's ability to modernize and develop politically in a complex and competitive world. Mexico's way out of its debt morass entails much more than a debt package.

The Debt Mirage: Mexico in the 1970s

During the 1970s, Mexico's foreign debt helped to prop up its shaky domestic economy. Until the late 1960s, Mexico's economy had been sound. Its growth was high by international standards; agricultural exports financed imports of the necessary industrial inputs and stable monetary and fiscal policies provided a friendly environment for investment and savings. It was easy to be prosperous.

By the late 1960s, however, agricultural exports began to decline, as a growing population absorbed an ever larger share of a declining domestic production. In 1965, Mexico still exported grains, including maize, its dietary staple. By 1970, Mexico had become a grain importer, and still is today. Although Mexico could not sustain economic growth without fundamental changes, the government had to operate within a precarious political balance following the bloody crushing of the student movement in 1968.

The 1970s were supposed to have been a decade of reform. Had all forecasts materialized, economic growth would have plummeted and immediate economic reform would have been inevitable. Instead, after 1973, the Arab oil embargo gave the government an unprecedented source for debt financing, petrodollars, while it paid lip service to reform. The government presence in the economy grew rapidly as it acquired and created (often unprofitable and inviable) businesses, increased imports, and introduced endless subsidies for firms and workers, the middle class, and bureaucrats. The availability of foreign currency made most people discount any need for reform. Foreign credit looked like a permanent (and free) source of wealth.

In 1982, reality came home to roost. During the first half of the year, putting together new syndicated loans became increasingly difficult. Mexico had become so addicted to foreign credit and loans were becoming so large that only groups of banks rather than individual institutions could float them. As world oil prices began to fall in 1981, decreasing the value of oil exports, the banks became skeptical about Mexico's viability. By August 1982, they decided not to roll over any more short-term loans. The Mexican government had made no provision for such a contingency, was caught off guard, and was forced to default on its debt obligations. Furthermore, in a rush to find scapegoats, the government took over the private banking system.

The Politics of Debt: From "Adjustment" to "Reform"

In December 1982, Miguel de la Madrid was sworn in as president. In a break with tradition, his inaugural address consisted of a specific, clear-cut program to deal with economic chaos instead of the usual philosophical outline of the new administration's vision. His first aim was to stabilize the economy and reduce inflation (then 400 percent annually). In 1983, his draconian program cut inflation to 80 percent, halved the fiscal deficit (to 8.5 percent of GDP), and reversed the trade deficit to a surplus.

The success of this Immediate Program for Reordering the Economy was short-lived, based on the wrong assumptions. First, the program aimed at reducing or overturning the fiscal and trade deficits. It succeeded on both counts, but through policies that could not initiate an economic recovery: it lowered the fiscal deficit by virtually eliminating investment, increasing taxes, and containing current expenditures (mainly wages). The deficit was reduced, but at the price of postponing economic recovery. The bureaucracy and the network of political interests around government were not touched. As strategy, containment failed, as it had to: every budgetary restriction was met by political pressures to increase spending, which, ultimately, paid off. A similar principle was applied to the trade deficit: imports were restricted but no export-promotion drive was attempted at a time when the U.S. market appeared ready and willing to buy anything. The import cutoff, like the lid on investment in infrastructure, spelled economic stagnation.

To justify the adjustment program, government blamed foreign debt and foreign banks. The banks were sitting ducks because debt was being serviced at the expense of domestic spending. No politician would discuss the possibility that the structure of the economy had to change, not for the sake of servicing debt but in order to attain a sustainable recovery. For their part, the foreign bankers assumed that they had done no wrong, even though many (if not most) of their loans had been made for projects that, with the collapse of oil and steel prices, had ceased to be economically or financially viable. Each side blamed the other.

In 1983, for the first time in its modern history, Mexico experienced a depression. Purchasing power of the average salary dropped more than 45 percent and GDP declined 5 percent. Unemployment showed little increase, however, because the labor impact of the recession fell mainly on the underemployed (people who lack skills for jobs in a modern economy). The income effects, ironically, fell mostly on the middle class, the largest beneficiaries of subsidies (for staples, drinking water, public transportation, and the like).

Despite a modest economic recovery in 1984, the Immediate Program for Reordering the Economy collapsed early in 1985. Inflation settled in at about 50 percent a year, and the economy again slipped into recession. Within the administration, infighting over economic policy was constant. Some policymakers argued for repudiating foreign debt; others urged profound economic reform. Trade policy was one area of interminable dispute even after the initial gains. The critical connection between trade and debt should have been obvious: as long as trade policy remained extremely restrictive, debt could never be serviced. By the same token, an open trading regime could reduce debt relative to a country's growing wealth.

The economic argument was straightforward, but the debate was political, bureaucratic, and circuitous. Trade policymakers benefited enormously from their discretionary powers under the restrictive trading regime. Furthermore, their constituencies—the bureaucracy and industry—supported them for fear of foreign competition and loss of their wealth-generating status quo. As the economy deteriorated and still another foreign crisis gripped Mexico in mid-1985, the Immediate Program was superseded by one of the most ambitious reforms ever undertaken by a developing country. The de la Madrid administration took an entirely different approach to economic policy. It began to privatize government-owned corporations, drop old promonopolistic regulations, and continue the squeeze on public finances. Most significant for real and sustainable reductions in government spending, the new government began, in earnest, to eliminate government departments and entities. Since 1985, the government has privatized close to 1,500 companies out of the 2,000 total. Budget cuts amount to almost 10 percent of GDP—more than triple the original (tougher) Gramm-Rudman budget reduction package in the United States.

This new set of policies was tantamount to revolution. The old policies responded to well-established constituencies that benefited from monopolies, monopolistic practices, and discretionary powers wielded by the bureaucracy. The new policies corresponded to a different concept of world reality and a clear political calculation that the "old order" was politically and socially unsustainable. The reformers recognized that Mexico could not remain aloof from events in the rest of the world and that economic stagnation would eventually destroy the traditional political system. The new domestic order would require a strong, growing, and internationally competitive economy to raise living standards at home. Absent these conditions, the days of the "old order" were numbered. Reform was preferable to instability even if it entailed political changes to the snug old realm of vested interests. For the government coalition, the costs of any short-term dislocation were minuscule next to the overwhelming costs of standing pat.

In the historical context of the day, the administration's vision and commitment become paramount. In Peru, President Alan García had virtually repudiated his country's debt, with no apparent reprisals, while Mexico pursued an orthodox adjustment program over popular objections. Not until 1990, when Peru's economic situation became desperate and Mexico was already on the path to strong recovery, did the "easy way out" begin to lose popular appeal in Mexico.

To de la Madrid and later Carlos Salinas de Gortari, economic recovery was a political imperative. High population growth in Mexico puts dramatically different economic demands on that government than it does in countries with stable populations such as Venezuela or Argentina. With more than half its people under fifteen years of age, Mexico will have to create about a million new jobs a year for the next fifteen years. Economic growth and job creation are political imperatives if Mexico is to avert potentially uncontainable social instability.

For most Mexicans, the fact that many hindrances to economic recovery were being dismantled was of little relevance or interest. Few understood or cared about subtle policy arguments; most cared only about tangible benefits of economic growth. But the problem went deeper. The nature of the reform ran counter to decades of indoctrination about the benefits of state-led development. Furthermore, the people who stood to lose from the reform—mainly the bureaucracy and some key unions—realized its thrust and, in the presidential election campaign of 1988, began to exploit the state-led development tradition to their political advantage.

Too late—four years into an economic reform that had yet to benefit the population at large—the de la Madrid administration understood that the political link was missing from the reform equation. Reform had eroded the power base of the Institutional Revolutionary Party (PRI) after more than six decades of rule. Many traditional PRI constituencies organized against Carlos Salinas de Gortari, the candidate that stood for the reform. Cuauhtémoc Cárdenas, son of a former Mexican president who had set the statist course of Mexico's development in the 1930s, succeeded in organizing an odd coalition of affected vested interests: labor (particularly teachers' unions and unions representing some government-owned corporations, such as Pemex), the left, the urban poor, and a large segment of the intelligentsia. While the race was close, Salinas won the much-disputed election. The 1988 election marked the beginning of the end of an unchallenged PRI, inaugurating a new era in Mexico's politics.

For the new administration, the political logic of reform had never been so clear. Reform had gone too slowly to garner any benefits and had given the opposition time to organize and fight it. The 1988 elections held two lessons. One was that reform could not succeed unless it dismantled the vested interests that hindered it. Miguel de la Madrid had attempted to avoid direct hits on those interests in the hope that the benefits of reform would make the opposition irrelevant. The other lesson had to do with the nature of the political system—inward-looking, a parallel to the closed and protected economy. As the economy opened up, a new political arrangement was needed to go with the newly competitive economy.

Salinas wasted no time. Reform had become politically urgent. Whereas de la Madrid had weighed the political costs of not reforming against the theoretical costs of dislodging vested interests, the issue had ceased to be academic for Salinas. The political costs had been paid in the presidential election. Reform was, in the administration's view, the only way to economic recovery.

Salinas launched a three-pronged strategy. The first thrust was against the vested interest groups blocking reform. During his first few months in office, Salinas prosecuted corrupt labor and business leaders and a few politicians, signaling what he wanted to accomplish and what his opposition could expect. His second strategy was to accelerate and deepen the reform. He undertook massive deregulation, eliminated investment deterrents, pursued his predecessor's anti-inflationary program (which had reduced inflation from nearly 200 percent to about 20 percent annually), and launched new debt-reduction negotiations with the banks. On the political front, he built an impressive coalition, including most of the constituencies that had composed the heart of Cárdenas's political base in 1988.

Salinas wanted the banks to accept part of the burden by reducing their debt-servicing charges. His target had ceased to be debt itself, but rather the obsession with debt that deflected foreign investment and kept domestic savings too low. Hence, although the actual reduction in the flow of debt servicing was small (less than 20 percent of total servicing), Salinas succeeded in eliminating the psychological debt issue as the centerpiece of debate in Mexico.

Consolidating the Reform

Deciding upon and beginning reform is one thing; consolidating it is quite another. Mexicans have learned to live with inflation, governmental policy shifts, and uncertainty. After more than two decades of this deadly mix, government credibility is not an abundant commodity. For reform to succeed, Salinas had to find a way to guarantee its viability; his decision to pursue a free trade agreement with the United States was made with exactly that goal in mind.

Mexico's government faces a series of dilemmas involving standards of living and eliminating the last vestiges of inflation, settling trade disputes with the United States—our largest trading partner—and reorganizing the political system. These challenges entail enormous risks and demand clear vision. The political viability of Mexico's current government is at stake as well as reform.

For five years now, the economic indicators have shown slow but steady improvement. Yet reform is only relevant—and politically viable—to the extent that it improves the standard of living. If it does not, any notion of reform becomes meaningless. To resolve the first dilemma, the Mexican government has to make reform deliver its promised benefits.

The pre-debt Mexican economy grew 6 percent a year. Most sectors grew evenly, protected from imports; domestic demand was more or less even for all sectors. Whether business invested in one sector or another didn't matter; success was almost a sure thing, diversification was not too risky, and few firms went bankrupt. Similarly, workers could take almost any kind of job.

Open to competition, success is no longer certain. The risk of failure comes as a surprise to people used to manufacturing and selling everything at home, regardless of quality, cost, or efficiency, and protected from outside competition. Growth and employment are increasingly determined by each company's ability to compete in foreign as well as domestic markets, not by government spending. Some succeed; others do not.

Mexican industry's first challenge today is survival; becoming competitive comes later. As trade barriers fall, Mexico is likely to have many fewer industries than in the past. The gamble is that those that survive will become globally competitive. The process of change along these lines is already apparent in the virtual disappearance of some sectors and rapid growth of others, but it will take years to consolidate.

Mexico faces a relatively small problem of unemployment (3–4 percent a year at worst); its big problem is underemployment (20 percent of the economically active population). The transformation of industry and agriculture is therefore unlikely to affect employment levels. Mexico's long-term stability, however, depends on training and educating the children of today's underemployed for assimilation into the labor force. This assumes that once the ranks of the employable grow, the economy will need them—in other words, that reform will be completely successful.

A basic tenet of reform is economic liberalization. This means that anybody can import virtually anything.[3] Again, this means success for some, failure for others. The new competitive environment will have dramatic repercussions. First, wages will grow much faster in prosperous sectors than in the less successful ones. Second, many firms will face bankruptcy and layoffs. And third, despite bankruptcies and adjustments, a very large part of industry will make it. The results to date support reform, but mostly at the microlevel. Successful exporters, for example, have increased real wages every year for the last four years, and many firms have recovered and added to the real wage level of the early 1980s. Another point of evidence is the rise in manufactured exports from less than $4 billion in 1985 to slightly over $17 billion in 1990.

Despite strong industrial signs that reform is paying off, the standard of living has not improved much at grass roots. When will the people see results? Will reform succeed in the numbers, but fail at the political level? These are not idle questions. To the extent that the majority perceives that reform is beginning to deliver, it will be successful. In the process, inflation will play a major role.

Inflation reached an all-time high of over 400 percent a year in late 1982, and after years of fiscal adjustment, peaked again in 1987. The anti-inflation program begun by de la Madrid and continued by Salinas brought inflation down to the mid-20 percent level by 1990. Politically, this program has worked because recession has been avoided. The economy has grown at an average of 4 percent a year, about 2 percent in per capita terms, since 1987. Though not extraordinary, this rate of growth has allowed jobs to be created and incomes to rise. But price controls over key raw materials and staples have been a major component of the anti-inflation program. Eliminating these controls will be politically ticklish if prices rise much, but many businesses claim their investment projects are being halted pending the removal of price controls.

Ideologically, the anti-inflation program collides head-on with reform, which stands for the elimination of artificial restraints on competition. The administration's first challenge now is to remove remaining price controls, upsetting prices as little as possible in the process. Nevertheless, the reform will most likely withstand the immediate inflationary impact of their removal because both seek the same end result—fiscal equilibrium. The key to the government's inflation policy is that it is gradual. Thus, although the results may be less impressive in the short term, they are likely to be lasting.

The second challenge is more political in nature. Perseverance and consistency will be needed during the transition to a modern economy, because all parties will have to make enormous adjustments and only some of them will succeed. Reform, the administration's only viable economic policy, is not necessarily the easiest political course. Pressures to increase spending are relentless. Old hardliners often try to recover lost territory through "informal" regulations, while other interests sometimes pursue short-term gains at the expense of reform.

This is not Mexico's first attempt at economic reform. Governments since the early 1970s have tried but failed to garner enough political power to dislodge political and economic interests entrenched in the status quo. The debt crisis was one devastating result of capitulating to these pressures. In the mid-1980s, when Mexico was facing recession and clamorous demands from across the economy and the political spectrum, the political dilemma became obvious and the trade-offs transparent. It was recognized that going after vested interests would initially create instability but that not dealing with them would make reform impossible, thus assuring protracted instability. Hence, for the last two Mexican governments, the logic of reform followed a profoundly political rationale. In other words, Mexico's economic reform is largely the result of political realities and political calculations.

Completing this reform and restoring economic growth in an open economy is a political imperative for the Salinas administration. Negotiating a free trade agreement with the United States corresponds to this political imperative as well as to Mexico's economic interests. The economic rationale is the natural extension of the reform process: securing a market for Mexico's goods, eliminating nontariff barriers to Mexico's exports, reducing the high U.S. tariffs that limit Mexico's access to the United States, and creating a two-sided mechanism for the resolution of trade disputes. Once Mexico decided to open up its markets and enhance its industrial competitiveness, the single most important hindrance to reform became the lack of certainty that Mexico would have access to its major (and largest) export market, the United States. From Mexico's vantage point, the economic rationale for the free trade agreement was to make domestic economic reform viable.

Because economic reform had deep political underpinnings to begin with, the free trade agreement also has a major political content. Economic reform in Mexico signifies a dramatic shift in policy. After decades of serving the interests of a handful, economic reform represents a break with the past and a redefinition of political alliances and constituencies that keep the governing coalition in power. The cement holding the new coalition together is the expectation of economic recovery and a redistribution of its benefits among the coalition partners. The coalition includes large segments of the middle class and of the rising "popular" classes, including most of the working class. For all of these groups, the free trade agreement guarantees the permanence of economic reform and the viability of the coalition. Furthermore, a free trade agreement, cast in concrete, would depoliticize economic reform.

Since the 1988 elections had been marred by accusations of fraud, the results of the August 1991 federal elections were crucial to Salinas's reform efforts. And they did exactly what they had to do. They gave the president an almost unqualified mandate to pursue reform. The Mexican people supported Salinas overwhelmingly; they also showed the growing sophistication of Mexican voters. Most people voted without the least regard for the traditional structures of power, revealing the dramatic political as well as economic effects of the reform. The ongoing trade negotiations with the United States and Canada are likely to be critical to the consolidation of this process.

For Mexico, therefore, the proposed free trade agreement encompasses a critical political component. The conclusion of an agreement would serve as a political guarantee to every group involved in the governing coalition as well as to business—domestic and foreign—which bears the enormous responsibility for effecting economic recovery.

Alternative Scenarios

Clearly, Mexico's government has a tremendous stake in the success of the proposed free trade agreement. Since the Salinas administration is not the first to attempt reform and all previous attempts have failed, the political capital at risk in this venture is enormous. Not for eight decades has a Mexican government ventured so far as the present one toward tightening the country's economic and political relationship with the United States. Considering Mexico's uneasy history with the United States, the Salinas administration is assuming huge political risks. Two questions come to mind in this regard. One involves the central issue of political change in Mexico. The other has to do with the risks of failure and the kind of political scenario that may result from a successful negotiation.

The Salinas administration is, after all, a direct heir of single-party governments since 1929. This raises the question of political change. Wouldn't frequent change of parties in government be worth encouraging? some observers wonder. Others suggest that negotiations for a free trade agreement should be used as an instrument of political change in Mexico. While Mexico and Mexicans would benefit from an alternation of parties in government, the timing of this discussion is paradoxical: not in sixty years have Mexico and Mexicans experienced as much political change as they have since reform began in 1985.

Political change is the main feature of Mexican society today. Economic reform has altered relationships between groups and individuals. A few examples might illustrate the depth of this change. Unions, for instance, were once led by "leaders" appointed by labor federations. Today import competition has forced each union to negotiate head on with its own employer. Democratic election of new leaders has been one result. Today labor and management are working together to increase productivity in order to survive. This would have been unimaginable a little while ago.

Signs of an opening up can be seen everywhere. Bureaucrats have lost access to privileged information and, as a result of deregulation, can no longer slow down policy implementation. Consumers have a wide choice of products in supermarkets. Sooner or later, people are going to demand a similar range of choices at work, at school, at city level. Recent developments in Guanajuato and San Luis Potosí, two Mexican states where the PRI was declared winner in the gubernatorial race but then had to withdraw its victorious candidates to appease the opposition, show the breathtaking pace of political change. It would not be an exaggeration to say that elections will most likely not be the source of conflict or fraud in the future; not only are there no more incentives for anyone to misbehave in elections, but the costs of electoral fraud are becoming unbearable for the PRI and for the government. In other words, political change is already a reality. Soon a political vision similar to the one driving the economic reform will have to emerge to institutionalize political changes.

In this context, the free trade agreement is much more crucial to Mexico's long-term development and stability than it is to the United States or Canada. Failure to conclude an agreement would deal a severe blow to the Salinas administration and to economic reform. The administration's policy of cooperation with the United States would be a certain casualty. Failure of the agreement would strengthen the cluster of political groups that have traditionally been suspicious of U.S. motives. Mexico could not return to the prereform era, but anti-reform political parties and groups within the PRI would try to contain it and revert to isolationism.

The problem, however, is not one of policy preferences. The Salinas administration did not embark on reform and free trade agreement negotiations as an intellectual exercise, but in recognition of the fact that Mexico's prereform economy could not provide its growing population with a livelihood. Since any attempt to roll back reform now would be likely to curtail economic growth and improvements in living conditions, and might even lead Mexico back down the road to the instability of the early 1980s, the reform would probably stay in place. Its dynamism, however, could easily evaporate. The point is that with or without a free trade agreement, to attain global competitiveness and maintain domestic stability, Mexico has to go on with economic and political reform.

The opposite scenario—a successful free trade agreement—would enhance the Salinas administration and add momentum to reform.

Mexico could then assume its full role in the large, emergent market in North America, the only one of the world's three major economic centers that is not yet formally integrated.

Mexico's Debt in Perspective

Mexico's transformation is ongoing. The odds of success look good, but the jury is still out, and plenty could go wrong. The next few years will see whether this reform is viable over the long haul. One way or another, Mexico will become an example of a winner or a loser.

Whatever the result, Mexico's experience with reform and debt in the 1980s prompts assorted conclusions by different observers. Many an author sees the 1980s as a "lost decade" because most social and economic indicators deteriorated and development slowed down at least a decade. For Mexico, the debt crisis proved to be an ill-resolved, but not unsolvable, policy problem.

Debt is a policy problem to the extent that misguided policies lead to too much debt for too many uneconomic investment projects, or, worse, for improper purposes. Banks and governments are equally responsible for these mistakes. Once the debt bomb exploded and highly indebted nations defaulted, debt became a different type of policy problem, but most governments tried to solve it by doing more of the same thing. Following the same old policies, instead of looking for the causes of so much indebtedness, made most countries still poorer and less creditworthy. When Mexico shifted its basic policy approach, economic recovery and debt servicing became possible and compatible.

Many Latin American nations, including the three largest economies (Brazil, Mexico, and Argentina), ended the debt boom era with much more debt than they could digest. Rotten policies had led to the point where not even the best rescue package could undo the fact of too much debt on the books that nobody could service. The banks were right all along: overhauling every Latin American economy was the only way out of the mess, even if their motives were less than altruistic. For the banks, any argument was the right one if it spared their shareholders from shouldering the weight of solution. (Never mind that the debt mess could not have happened without the compliance of the banks and their experts.)

The past decade abounds with lessons about debt. Only recently has it become accepted that the assumptions behind both the banks' lending and the government borrowing were incompatible with what was happening in the world economy. While the banks ferreted out customers to "recycle" petrodollars, countries like Japan were still busier improving their own industrial efficiency. In the meantime, the banks were lending money for projects that, even if well conceived (and many were not), were rapidly becoming irrelevant because of events elsewhere. Although the banks were lending dollars and expected to be paid back in dollars, their key loan criteria did not stipulate that the loans had to go to dollar-generating projects.

Ill-conceived decisions by all parties in the 1970s led to the debt crisis of the 1980s. Judging by recent experience, only close cooperation between governments and banks can do away with the debt issue as a problem. Much of the debt was poorly invested, but much of it is backed by assets that are still there, even if they are probably worth less than the liabilities incurred to acquire them. These investments could be made profitable if banks and governments would throw out the obsolete concept of sovereign credit and handle the problem like any other creditor-debtor relationship.

With economic reform, Mexico has managed to get a somewhat positive response from the banking community, and debt no longer looks insurmountable. With the success of Mexico's reform, the whole theory of development may have to be reconsidered. The traditional path to development[4] was based on the assumption that "infant-industry" protection and a strong government hand in the economy were keys to economic development. To the extent that liberalization, privatization, deregulation, and freer markets work in Mexico, the development concept will have to look different in the future.

In Mexico today, much more than a theory is at stake. The reform process touches the lives of every Mexican; it also affects prospects for stability throughout the North American region. The outcome of Mexico's reform has implications well beyond Mexico's borders.

Notes

1. Economic data used in this chapter are drawn from the following sources: Banco de México, *Indicadores del Sector Externo*, cuaderno mensual (various issues). Instituto Nacional de Estadistica Geografia e Informática, *Estadisticas del Comercio Exterior de México* (various years). Nacional Financiera, *La economía mexicana en cifras*, (México: Nafinsa, 1990). Banco de México, *Indicadores Económicos, 1991* (Información Mensual, Anual e Histórica).

2. Total foreign debt in 1982 was $88 billion, compared to $92 billion in 1990. As a percentage of GDP, debt represented 51 percent in 1982, compared to 40.8 percent in 1990. Debt service declined from 51 percent of exports in 1982 to 34 percent in 1990. Because exports are one of the main elements driving Mexico's recovery, their composition is crucial and reveals the depth of change in the Mexican economy. In particular, oil exports accounted for 71 percent of total exports in 1982, compared to 38 percent in 1990.

3. Two exceptions remain: agriculture, where import permits are required, and automobiles, which can be imported only by manufacturers.

4. I refer here to the development model articulated in the 1950s by the U.N. Economic Commission for Latin America.

MEXICO: ECONOMIC STATISTICS

	1986	1987	1988	1989	1990	1991e
Domestic Economy						
Real GDP (1980 pesos, billions)	4,739	4,820	4,889	5,041	5,236	5,424
% change	-3.7	1.7	1.4	3.1	3.9	3.6
Per capita GDP (US$)	1,626	1,729	2,103	2,459	2,760	3,071
Per capita real GDP (% change)	-5.7	-0.3	-0.6	0.6	2.4	2.1
Inflation (% change)	86.2	131.8	114.2	20.0	26.7	22.5
Population (millions)	79.57	81.20	82.84	84.89	86.15	87.80
Unemployment (% of labor force)	4.3	3.9	3.6	2.9	2.5	na
Public sector borrowing (% of GDP)	16.5	16.0	12.4	5.5	3.5	1.3

Mexico: Economic Statistics

	1986	1987	1988	1989	1990	1991e
External Economy (US$, millions)						
Exchange rate (average peso–US$)	612	1,378	2,273	2,475	2,821	3,018
Merchandise exports	16,031	20,656	20,565	22,842	26,951	27,250
Merchandise imports	-11,432	-12,223	-18,898	-25,438	-31,090	-38,150
Trade balance	4,599	8,433	1,667	-2,596	-4,139	-10,900
Current account balance	-1,673	3,966	-2,443	-5,912	-6,368	-12,600
Total external debt	105,287	110,901	100,893	97,779	106,942	117,435
% of GDP	81.4	79.0	57.9	46.8	45.0	42.5
% of exports goods, services & income	444.4	370.9	315.2	271.3	256.0	271.0
Total debt service	12,667	12,645	14,994	15,696	15,014	14,847
% of exports goods, services & income	53.5	42.3	46.8	43.5	35.9	34.3

e estimate

Source: The Institute of International Finance

7 / The Brazilian Quandary Revisited

Marcílio Marques Moreira

In recent years, Brazilians have turned the once-common phrase "Brazil is the land of the future," into a somewhat disillusioned joke: "Brazil is—and always will remain—the land of the future!" In 1986, even though Brazil was already ensnared in the debt crisis, many Brazilians remained confident that the rapid growth that began in the late 1960s would surge again and that the future would indeed soon arrive. Thus, in *The Brazilian Quandary*, undaunted by the country's setbacks, I wrote that Brazil was "poised at the edge of a major economic breakthrough."[1] For a number of reasons, that breakthrough did not materialize. But I am convinced that it is still on the horizon. In fact, dramatic changes for the better in policies, practices, and the way people think make its appearance seem even imminent.

Democratic Consolidation

Many changes have occurred since 1986. The new Constitution of 1988 provides for a type of broad participatory democracy unprecedented in Brazil's history. Elections the following year marked Brazilians' first free and direct vote for president since the 1961 election of Janio Quadros.[2] These important political advances were made despite the frailty of Brazil's party system and the backdrop of deepening economic crisis.

The 1989 election brought an energetic and determined forty-year old, Fernando Collor, to the presidency with 35 million votes (53 percent of the valid ballots). Collor presented the nation with a modern agenda aimed at radically reforming both Brazil's economy and its political structure. He also put forth sweeping plans to take on issues ranging from environmental pollution to the social debt owed to poor Brazilians, who generally have not benefited from their country's economic progress.

With that election, Brazil and its 146 million people became the world's third largest democracy (after India and the United States), and perhaps one of the more stable. Brazil is relatively free of ethnic, religious, and nationalistic tensions at home and has no outside threats, border feuds, regional rivalries, or other disputes with its neighbors. Such remarkable political progress is hard to fully appreciate from abroad. Unfortunately, economic and social progress lag behind, and a rapid restructuring of the world economy may pose as yet unclear threats to Brazil's development.

The Economic Environment

In the two years since he took office, Collor has remade Brazil's economic environment: inflation has been brought largely under control, the state has begun to deregulate and sell off its industries, and foreign debt has been renegotiated. After an initial sharp drop in GDP, growth has stabilized. These changes follow decades of economic upheaval, marked by periods of rapid growth and high inflation giving way to periods of sharp decline.

After reaching annual rates above 10 percent in the "miracle years" between 1968 and 1973, GDP growth lost momentum. Then, in the 1980s, economic growth barely matched the increase in population, giving this period the label of the "lost decade." Many factors contributed to the stagnation: exhaustion of the import substitution model of industrialization; the burden of domestic and foreign debt; the inefficiency of the government sector and, especially, of public enterprises; and the failure of stabilization programs to control higher inflation.

Yet Collor inherited a country that was relatively well off. In 1991, Brazil's GDP reached nearly $400 billion, or roughly $2,500 on a per capita basis. This placed Brazil among the "upper-middle-income developing countries," according to World Bank criteria.

Inflation

High inflation has been a feature of Brazil's economy for more than a quarter century, and for a long time it coexisted with rapid growth. But the stagnation of the "lost decade" showed how the uncertainty and instability resulting from high inflation had come to discourage investment, seriously damaging the economy. By the mid-1980s, stabilization became the major goal of economic policy. Yet the fight against inflation, despite five stabilization programs in the last six years, has been particularly frustrating.

From 1986 until early 1991, Brazil opted for so-called heterodox shocks. These programs began with a wage and price freeze designed to stop inflationary momentum, and were followed by classical policies aimed at curbing the government deficit and monetary expansion. This second and most important phase, however, either failed completely (as in 1986, 1987, and 1989) or was only partially implemented (as in 1990 and 1991).

After inflation reached 80 percent a month in March 1990, the new government unveiled a stabilization package that went beyond past efforts. It included stiff taxes on financial assets and even the seizure of some assets for up to 30 months. Tax collections were increased and expenditures cut, enabling the government to reduce the public sector deficit from 7.3 percent of GDP in 1989 to 2.2 percent in 1991. Annual inflation dropped from 1,783 percent in 1989, to 1,476 percent in 1990, and 480 percent in 1991.

Brazil's government has managed to keep the monetary and financial system intact despite the impact of high inflation and the recurrent threat of hyperinflation—not a mean accomplishment under prevailing economic conditions. Many observers credit this to the extensive use of indexation. From the mid-1960s through the 1970s, savings, investment, and growth continued despite high inflation because indexation helped the economy withstand inflation's pernicious side effects, such as erosion of the real value of assets. Indexation helped Brazil's economy grow 10 percent and exports to increase 40 percent, even during the relatively high inflation years from 1986 to 1990.

However, indexation was also blamed for the failure of the stabilization plans, as it tended to perpetuate past inflation as well as to feed new inflationary pressures back into the economy. Thus, when inflation reignited in early 1991 after the first Collor plan, the government moved to eliminate widespread indexation, particulary in contracts maturing in less than six months. Under partial deindexation, the persistence of inflation, even at levels once considered tolerable, severely threatens any stabilization program.

This new environment, together with real successes in reducing inflation and the government deficit, helps explain the government's continuing determination to stamp out still-resilient inflationary pressures. The government even has been willing to endure the cost of an unprecedented decline in GDP of 4 percent in 1990, with recovery estimated at only 1 percent in 1991. Inflation for the month of December 1991, however, crept back up to 23 percent. This is due to a combination of factors: a period of adjustment following the last price freeze, a devaluation, and a rise in agricultural prices due to smaller grain crops. Prices also have been spurred by expectations, based on previous experiences, of a new price freeze.

As the government has embraced fiscal reform and tight monetary policy and abandoned the idea of any new price freeze or other type of economic shock treatment, confidence in the new economic policy has been building and long-term inflationary expectations are receding. The new phase of the anti-inflation program has been supported, to a degree unheard of previously, by deep structural reforms. After facing legal and political obstacles, the privatization program is moving ahead, contributing to the overall effort to restructure the public sector. At the same time, the government is opening the economy to foreign competition by lowering tariffs and other trade barriers, encouraging the inflow of foreign capital, and reestablishing normal ties with the international financial system.

Further gains in stabilization will depend on the success of fiscal reform, for which the support of Congress is essential. To balance its finances and to promote economic modernization, the government has proposed many changes in legislation, including various constitutional amendments. The amendments aim to make it possible to introduce new taxes, cut certain protected expenditures, and increase control over the government's finances. They also support modernization of the economy, especially by opening up state monopolies, such as telecommunications, to competition with private firms, both Brazilian and foreign.

Overregulation

Low productivity is another of Brazil's chronic economic problems. Brazil's early development model promoted import substitution and market protection over competition and efficiency. All too often, special interest groups took possession of these protected areas and even managed to have their "rights of survival" written into the Constitution. It is not only bureaucrats in state-run enterprises who guard these anticompetitive strongholds. Professional associations, labor unions, and private businesses are equally stubborn. To preserve their entrenched positions, these assorted groups wield educational requirements, restrictive membership procedures, and a tangled multitude of other prerequisites. The resulting overregulation promotes entitlements over efficiency and stifles competition, creativity, and growth.

This mentality in opposition to open competition and free labor negotiations has converged with other, mainly nationalistic ideas that hold that Brazil needs to maintain national "sovereignty" in "strategic" areas such as computers, steel, oil, and telecommunications. These attitudes help explain the difficulties encountered by the government's ambitious privatization program. In this context, it is remarkable that after a one-month delay due to several court injunctions, the first privatization auction took place in October 1991 with the explicit support of the executive, legislative, and judicial branches. Privatization has also enjoyed an unsuspected degree of public support (69.3 percent), according to a recent survey by the research institute "Vox Populi."

Thus, in the last quarter of 1991 USIMINAS, the largest steel mill in Latin America, was auctioned off, followed by four other smaller enterprises. In each case, the sale price was significantly above the minimum set by the government. Moreover, the government has already decided to accelerate the privatization program in 1992 and beyond. The next auctions will involve large and medium companies in the steel, fertilizer, and petrochemical sectors, among others. The program is expected to yield at least 0.5 percent of GDP per year, to be used entirely to retire outstanding public debt.

Debt

Brazil's foreign debt as of June 1991 stood at $115.7 billion, of which $68.9 billion was owed to international banks. In absolute terms, Brazil carries more debt than any other country in the developing world, but in relative terms, the total debt is only about 30 percent of GDP.[3]

From the early 1980s on, Brazil has had problems servicing its foreign debt. Although this debt burden seemed likely to have been shed by now, it continues to exert a combination of pressures on the Brazilian economy: the need to devote a significant percentage of export earnings to debt service, an ongoing struggle with foreign commercial bank creditors, difficulty in attracting private capital, a negative fiscal impact because the debt is largely owed by the public sector, and pressure from international agencies to implement austere fiscal and monetary policies.

The attempt to manage the debt crisis began in December 1982, with stopgap agreements aimed only at recycling the debt. In an attempt to find a permanent solution, Brazil in 1986 and 1987 tried to negotiate a discount on the debt, but was rebuffed by its creditors. The United States, in particular, strongly opposed the idea.

A long-anticipated Multi-Year Agreement (MYRA) was finally reached in September 1988 but proved to be a case of "too little, too soon." The International Monetary Fund (IMF), the World Bank, Japan's Nakasone Fund, and commercial banks all refused to commit sufficient funds to the MYRA. The chief reason cited for this lack of support was Brazil's noncompliance with rigid IMF performance targets. (Uncertainty about the outcome of Brazil's presidential campaign also seems to have contributed to the unwillingness of these institutions to commit resources. This has led some observers to wonder whether international bureaucrats and financiers would feel more at ease with a political regime not subject to democratic alternations of power.) In 1989, just six months after the MYRA was signed, the United States incorporated the concept of debt reduction into the Brady plan.

Throughout the late 1980s, debt and inflation fed on each other. The savings from deep cuts in investment and domestic programs were cancelled out as domestic debt grew and the money supply expanded (through government purchases of foreign exchange from private exporters to service foreign debt). Expansionary pressures built up, especially in 1988, as cruzados were issued to cover the cost of hefty debt-equity deals.

The United States followed a different route to alleviate its own debt-generated fiscal and monetary pressures in the 1980s. It simply underwrote domestic debt on its own capital market with money from abroad, mainly Japan. Brazil does not have this option. Its capital market, though more active and better structured than those of most developing countries, is still too small, thin, and nearsighted.[4]

The fiscal and monetary implications of Brazil's indebtedness loom large. Brazil's debt is 90 percent publicly held, but an overwhelming portion of its exports (between 80 and 90 percent) come from the private sector. Unlike Mexico and Venezuela, where state-owned oil companies generate the major export and directly provide the state with foreign exchange, Brazil has been faced with the troublesome task of taking cruzeiros from an enfeebled public sector.[5] This is why in negotiations Brazil has emphasized how fiscal and monetary constraints limit its debt service capacity.

When the Brady plan was announced in March 1989, fiscal and monetary pressures had already increased inflation. The sense of impending disaster was aggravated by the perception that the 1988 debt agreement was insufficient to avoid an exchange collapse later in the year, despite some innovative features (such as exit bonds and more flexible waiver mechanisms).

Faced with this crisis psychology, in January 1989 the government launched its third anti-inflation program (the Summer plan), and spent the first part of the year trying to complete or supplement the 1988 MYRA. (Reopening the MYRA was viewed as an unrealistic route to debt-reduction benefits offered under the Brady plan.) When support failed to materialize by the second quarter of 1989, the government had to stop paying interest on its long- and medium-term debt to commercial banks. This decision was not made in a spirit of defiance. Brazil had repeatedly proposed, to no avail, a transitional agreement that might have assured continuity of payment. Instead, inflation resumed with a vengeance, an exchange crisis seemed imminent, and uncertainty spread as the presidential campaign moved into the more radical run-off phase.

The Collor Plan

Good luck and surprising determination on the part of the lame-duck financial authorities forestalled hyperinflation, although its threshold had been reached. When President Collor took office on March 15, 1990, inflation was running at 80 percent a month. The day after his inauguration, Collor introduced a bold stabilization program. Along with this, he proposed a set of broad reforms directed at modernizing Brazil's economic structure and its sclerotic, import-substituting, state-led, debt-financed development model.

The new government spent its first six months in office focusing on inflation and structural reform. Sweeping administrative reform redefined the government's economic role, and a new trade and industrial policy opened the economy to outside competition.

Negotiations with the IMF began in August 1990. In October 1990, Brazil began meeting with its commercial bank creditors in the hope of normalizing its strained relations with the international financial community. Like all previous rounds since 1982, these negotiations were painful, frustrating, and protracted. In May 1991, the vexing question of arrears was settled. Negotiations with the IMF were resumed in August and a letter of intent describing the economic program was presented to the Fund in December, opening the way for a "standby" agreement approved by the IMF's Board in January 1992. This at last clears the path to complete negotiations with private creditors as well as the official bilateral lenders assembled in the so-called Paris Club.

In any case, the debt burden still casts an inhibiting shadow of uncertainty over consumers, savers, investors, exporters, importers, traders, and producers. Between 1986 and June 1991, Brazil's foreign debt actually rose from $105 billion to $115.7 billion, despite the $50 billion in interest paid over those five and a half years.[6] To remove this burden, which continues to swallow our economic future, a speedy, comprehensive, and fair solution must be found—an agreement considered satisfactory by our creditors that does not impose an unbearable strain on Brazil but does renew its access to international credit. This is the only way Brazil can end the vicious circle in which debt service consumes savings and export earnings, dampens investment, fuels inflation, and erodes foreign and domestic confidence.

Trade

With its strong and diversified export base, Brazil has run a trade surplus since 1970 and now has the world's third largest surplus, after Japan and Germany. Analysts predict a surplus of $11 billion for 1991, roughly equal to the 1990 figure.[7]

The array of U.S.-Brazil trade disputes that peaked between September 1985 and June 1990[8] were for the most part defused when President Collor jettisoned Brazil's old import substitution model and moved toward broader participation in the world economy. This does not mean other issues have not arisen and will not continue to do so. Many "traditional" U.S. industries may come to feel threatened by imports from Brazil and seek remedy. For this, the U.S. Congress has armed the executive branch with an extensive arsenal—often in flagrant disregard of the General Agreement on Tariffs and Trade (GATT). That is why Brazil hopes the Uruguay Round, which may be nearing successful completion, will broaden and strengthen the multilateral reach of GATT. This will control the aggressive unilateralism of U.S. trade policy and provide a more effective venue for resolving trade disputes fairly and promptly. The Uruguay Round will also hopefully open up other important markets, such as the European Community (EC) and Japan, especially in the area of agriculture. Indeed, a thorough reform of the extremely protectionist EC agricultural policies is particularly necessary.

The ability to successfully export its products is becoming increasingly critical to Brazil, both as a means of solving the debt problem and as a way to promote the concept of free trade to its own people. Whereas the issue of resolving the debt problem looks backward to the accumulated debt burden and debt service, the issue of trade liberalization looks to the future. It would be ironic if Brazil's efforts toward freer trade were undermined by neoprotectionism in the same industrial countries that convinced us of the virtues of a market economy and open trade. This danger of national protectionism would only be compounded by the formation of regional trade megablocs, a likely outcome should the Uruguay Round fail.

The Environment

Debt and trade remain Brazil's major concerns, but new issues crowd the international agenda. Among these are drugs, human rights, and nonproliferation of weapons. But the most important for Brazil is the environment. Brazil houses about 70 percent of the Amazon river basin, location of the world's last largely untouched expanse of tropical rainforest. The Brazilian Amazon accounts for some 50 percent of Brazil's territory, roughly equal in size to half the continental United States. This forest is home to a third of all known plant and animal species and contains almost 20 percent of the world's running fresh water.

For centuries the Amazon loomed large in the Brazilian imagination. To some, it was an Eden, a garden of riches, and a potential "granary" of the world. Others saw it as a green hell, sanctuary to wild animals, poisonous snakes, savage cannibals, and fierce horse riding Amazon natives. Over time, the Amazon has proven a bit of each. Its real dangers and sheer size prevented all but perfunctory occupation and development by "civilized" people. Between discovery in 1500 and independence in 1822, the Portuguese created the first modern civilization in the tropics along Brazil's Atlantic coast. In the process, they almost destroyed the region known as the Mata Atlantica through intense agricultural development. But neither the Portuguese nor the Brazilians after them could manage to extend their civilization to the Amazon.[9] In fact, even after intense efforts to develop the region in the 1970s and 1980s, almost 92 percent of the Amazon rainforest is still intact.

The motives for the onslaught on the Amazon during the 1970s and 1980s are complex. DDT, chainsaws, bulldozers, and small aircraft are among the new instruments that aided this "conquest." The conquerors include southern cattle ranchers displaced by intensive soybean agriculture, disgruntled farmhands and urban workers looking for new beginnings as gold-miners, profiteers grabbing credit-subsidies and tax breaks, and military strategists drawn to an unpopulated wilderness. For overactive imaginations, the possibility of a capitalist (or Communist) conspiracy to seize the region justified preemptive occupation.

The onslaught against the Amazon peaked in 1987 and 1988.[10] These were years of particularly intense forest destruction driven by fear that subsidies to work the land would be revoked, a sequence of droughts that ruined productive land and led farmers to clear new tracts, and the imminence of the new Constitution with its promise of land reform and its threat of expropriation of large, "unproductive" tracts.

The 1988 murder of Chico Mendes, the charismatic leader of the rubber tappers and a hero of the rainforest preservation movement, quickly transformed him into a martyr for the ecological cause. Brazilians and nongovernmental organizations worldwide expressed outrage. The Brazilian government responded quickly and, just two years after the assassination, convicted and handed down stiff sentences to the murderer and his father who were the owners of the land Mendes wanted to preserve. This became a symbol of Brazil's new awareness of the need to preserve the environment and protect people against rural violence. It also marked the start of Brazil's transition to a new era of international cooperation.

The Brazilian government's decision to host the United Nations Conference on Environment and Development, scheduled to be held in Rio de Janeiro in June 1992, is evidence of this new attitude. The government is turning a potentially contentious issue into an opportunity for constructive cooperation. The preservation of the Amazon is not only a matter of immediate, direct concern to Brazil, it is also an area where Brazil can greatly help to preserve one of the world's most important and fragile ecologies against the ravages of industrial greed.

Debt-for-Nature Swaps

Too much attention has been devoted to debt-for-nature swaps. Under these, the government converts foreign debt instruments donated by private parties, usually nongovernmental organizations, into cruzeiros to be used for ecological projects (for example, preserving fragile areas for environmental reasons). This mechanism can be useful to fund some specific environmental preservation projects. But its use is limited because it confuses two disparate and complex problems—debt and environment. The following comparisons are illustrative of the differences between these two issues:

▲ The debt problem is transitory. Environmental issues will be with us for a long time to come.

▲ Debt is a financial problem. The environment is essentially part of the public household. Each issue responds to its own logic.

▲ Preserving the environment's balance requires massive assets. Debt, however, is on the liability side of the ledger. Swapping a liability for a need for assets makes no sense.

▲ Brazil's debt problem is more a domestic fiscal problem than a balance of payments issue. Swapping a foreign liability that matures many years hence for local currency to be issued in the short term would only aggravate the most critical dimension of the debt problem: the severe fiscal and monetary constraints under which the Brazilian government must operate. Any environmentally linked release of local currency would have to be scheduled over a long-term period to avoid inflationary pressures.

Two factors point out the need for a more broad-based solution. First, the debt problem has stripped developing countries of the cash and credit they need to take up the environmental challenge and has favored predatory practices to maximize mineral and agricultural exports. Thus, a sufficiently broad solution would enable debtor countries to play a more constructive role in the defense of the ecosystem. Second, the environmental challenge is too big to be solved by any one country. It will take international cooperation of all sorts, including concessional loans and cash grants for the environmental cause.[11]

It was on the basis of these arguments that Brazil in 1991 introduced a plan for debt-for-nature swaps. The program is limited to $100 million and every swap requires government approval. The debt is converted at face value but cash is not immediately issued. Rather, in exchange for the debt the government issues bonds in cruzeiros. The project then receives in cash only the 6 percent perpetual annual interest due on the bonds, calculated on the basis of the par value. Given the normal discounts in the market (at the moment of the writing about 70 percent), the actual annual interest is several times higher.

Social Issues

Many other issues confronting Brazil today, although basically domestic in nature, have a broad international dimension. In a world united by ever-faster communications networks and a growing international consciousness, few dramatic events or problems in any country escape attention, curiosity, compassion, or outrage.

Among Brazil's unsolved domestic problems are the plight of the remaining Indian tribes; the fate of abandoned street children; chronic rural and urban violence; and, in cities like Rio de Janeiro, drugs and their ties to organized crime. These problems challenge the ingenuity of Brazil's fledgling democratic society and strain its scarce resources.

To its credit, Brazil has been able to keep major coca leaf farming and processing out of its territory. As in the United States, only marijuana is grown domestically and none is known to be exported. Involvement by Brazilians in international drug trafficking has also been deterred by the constant vigilance of the widely respected federal police force. Brazil remains, nevertheless, a potential transit point for coca. This is especially true along its long, underpopulated and unguarded borders with Peru, Bolivia, and Colombia, the three main Andean sources of coca.

Education

Education is increasingly critical in today's information-driven economy, where the "return on human capital is rising relative to that on financial capital."[12] This problem is one Brazil, with its underdeveloped educational system, is finding a serious constraint on progress.[13] It is a drag on economic growth, a critical factor in our scandalously unequal distribution of income and wealth, and a bar to the country's full political development.

Brazil's educational shortcomings are not limited to a lack of technical training. They also encompass general education all the way down to primary levels. Although some progress has been made, the numbers are still dismal. Today relatively few Brazilians have completed eight years of general schooling—and that is an improvement over ten years ago. In that same period, illiteracy also dropped, although it remains at an unacceptable 18 percent.[14]

General education in Brazil is still deficient not only in absolute terms but in relative terms—compared, for example, to the effort being made in Asian countries, especially by the "four tigers" (Hong Kong, Korea, Singapore, and Taiwan). The high priority these countries put on education, not the openness of their markets, explains much of their superior performance when compared to Latin America.[15]

These considerations have led the Collor government to make education its top priority over the next few years. The government is acting together with state and local governments, in particular by establishing the Integrated Centers for Child Care (CIACS). Their purpose is to provide education, nutrition and health care, sports, cultural activities, and professional training during the eight-hour period of attendance.

Education at university level is also poor, even though the federal government spends almost 1 percent of GDP on the network of tuition-free universities. Obsolete rules, narrowly defined subjects, and the insufficient qualifications of new entrants all work to limit the fruits of so massive an investment. Since higher education is critical to the country's drive toward modernity, the government is determined to radically change the bleak reality of its universities. One plan is to give more administrative autonomy to the federal universities, while providing them with the resources to improve their teaching, research, and extension activities. At the graduate level, the government is supporting additional fellowship grants and establishing new courses addressed to the changing needs of the country.

Science and Technology

The weakness in formal education has been compounded by insufficient attention to scientific research and technological development. Less than 1 percent of GDP goes to research and development. In modern economies, the information component of goods and services overshadows the classical factors of production—capital, labor, and raw materials—meaning this lack of R&D has become a major threat to Brazil's productivity.

All the more worrisome, developing countries are running into new barriers to their acquisition of modern technology. When countries like Japan and Korea were buying or copying all sorts of technology all over the world, these barriers did not exist. Many of the restrictions reflect legitimate desires to protect innovative inventors, prevent the proliferation of weapons of mass destruction, or preserve hard-won commercial interests. But, in other instances, phrases such as "fair trade" in technology[16] or "dual-use" know-how can disguise another motive: the wish to defend entrenched commercial advantages by non-market means. Barriers erected on "fair trade" or "national security" may mask a desire to keep developing countries from entering the market as new competitors.[17] Newly industrializing countries (NICs) like Brazil should not have to pay this excessive price for being latecomers.

However, as a show of good faith, Brazil has already begun to address the need to protect intellectual property. A bill drawn up by the administration is being discussed in Congress, with great chances of approval. This protection is essential if Brazil is to attract much-needed foreign investment. But it is equally necessary as a way to reward domestic creativity and to develop the country's scientific and technological research capabilities.[18]

One particular danger Brazil must avoid, in conjunction with the other nations of the region, is a costly and wasteful arms race. We owe it to ourselves to be as responsive as possible to legitimate international concerns about the proliferation of nuclear, chemical, and biological weapons. Here, international concerns and Brazil's national interests coincide. These weapons are proscribed by the Brazilian constitution, do not correspond to government policy, and do not appeal to public opinion. This has led the present government to unilaterally renounce interest in so-called pacific testing of nuclear weapons, which is permitted by Latin America's nonproliferation treaty (The Treaty of Tlateloco). Brazil is also opening all its nuclear facilities to inspection by Argentina and, as of December 1991, has agreed to the full scope of safeguards drawn up by the International Atomic Energy Agency.

The Travails of Transition

After World War II, developing countries were routinely advised to reject communism, develop natural resources, and save and invest assiduously. Today, the advice is equally simple, though the content has changed. The indisputably sound formula now in fashion is: stick to democracy, embrace the free market, and put your house in order. Yet the distance between stark reality and this lofty ideal is seldom bridged. With a few strategic exceptions (Poland, Egypt, and the drug-exporting countries), the predominant attitude is to hold off on providing support until the countries in transition get their act together. If these countries do surmount their crises, international cooperation might be considered as a reward on the grounds that they "deserve" it. But generally the international lenders overlook a few factors: the breadth of the needed reforms, the depth and solidity of existing economic structures often built up over centuries, and the huge competition for available resources.

Contrary to standard wisdom, Brazil is not a house ready for redecoration, lacking only enough diligence and political will. Brazil is a house that needs a new foundation and a bigger frame—both at the same time. Only then will it be ready to redecorate. This is no small job.

A reference to the respective situations of Central Europe and Latin America is illustrative. Latin America's only recently heralded accomplishments in restoring democracy and market economies has been almost entirely overshadowed by the events that catapulted Eastern Europe into a similar process. The hurdles to be overcome in both regions are similar in many ways, and radically diverse in many others.

In the case of Brazil, sheer size is the first difference. There are 146 million Brazilians spread over more land than West and East Europe combined. Moreover, Brazil's population is much younger, which means its needs are very different. The second difference is the bases of Brazilian society and economy, which in many ways are more primitive than those in Eastern Europe. Though Eastern Europe has lived under a military-authoritarian regime for twice as long as Brazil, state domination of the Brazilian economy and society goes back even further. The Portuguese legacy of a heavy state hand in economic and social life was largely untouched by the modernizing winds of the Renaissance and the Enlightenment.[19] In Central Europe, by contrast, state predominance was in large part imposed after World War II.

Brazil's retention of certain quasifeudal traits did not preclude a more modern economic approach. Many firms, for instance, managed against all odds to emerge from the crisis of the 1980s with solid finances, up-to-date equipment and management, lean design, and improved productivity. But this modern segment of the economy contrasts starkly with the still widespread traditional business mentality.

There is another critical difference. Brazilian society cannot be understood without reference to the deep imprint left by slavery.[20] The dimensions of slavery in Brazil were staggering: the country "imported" seven times the number of slaves taken to the United States, and slavery was not abolished until 1888.

Enormous disparities in income and wealth are another facet of Brazil's somber social reality that distinguishes it from Eastern Europe. That is why, although the state's role must be profoundly redefined it cannot simply be reduced to a "minimal state" as preached by free marketeers. The market economy Brazil pursues must develop wealth for all Brazilians.

Finally, although the big push to modernity is mainly in Brazil's hands, the country cannot do it alone. Because a modern "national" economy must be part of the world system,[21] its success depends also on a friendly international environment. Brazil is therefore committed to working to create a post-cold war international order that fully integrates Brazil and other developing nations both politically and economically.[22]

International Financial Markets

Besides the burden of foreign debt, Brazil must also look at the role foreign capital should play in domestic development. Should Brazil try to attract direct investment, bank loans, stock market equity, or newer financial instruments? What about the future of international coordination of macroeconomic policy, exchange levels, and interest rates? How can Brazil begin to take on its responsibilities as the world's ninth largest economy?[23]

Stuck in the second-class tier of the financial market, Brazil has lost control over its own assets and liabilities and has been unable to benefit from the global financial market. As do all heavily indebted developing countries, Brazil suffers from other serious imbalances as well, such as a massive hemorrhaging of capital. One effect of the debt crisis was a sudden reversal of the usual North-South flow of financial resources. A heavy stream of payments went North to refinance the debt at the same time as commodity prices faltered, markets contracted, and oil prices shot up. Capital also flowed South to North as large private debt amortizations reduced the region's overall exposure and as investors sought safe refuge and "optimum returns." Only in 1990 did the first signs of reversal of this trend appear.[24]

Fortunately, capital flight out of Brazil never reached the levels of other Latin American countries, where it fed the debt-accumulation process. Moreover, there are recent signs that some flight capital is now returning. On the other hand, legitimate capital outflow has grown lately as large Brazilian corporations invest abroad, usually in search of improved access to markets and technology. In 1991, however, this outflow was more than matched by a renewed inflow as more than $10 billion of foreign capital was invested in diverse projects.

The large balance-of-payments deficit in the United States and the corresponding surpluses in Japan, Germany, Taiwan, and elsewhere have introduced a troubling uncertainty to the international financial environment. There have been rapid gyrations in interest rates, sudden movements of large amounts of capital, and wild swings in exchange rates. Tariff reductions won over years of negotiations or competitive advantages gained by intense cost-cutting efforts can disappear overnight. Surges in key currencies like the U.S. dollar spill over to countries like Brazil, whose currencies are pegged to the dollar as a way to provide some modicum of stability.

Some of these developments in the financial market are negative, some promising. As a nation, Brazil is concerned about imbalances that could aggravate its predicament, but it remains hopeful about the opportunities available once the debt burden is reduced.

One World or Several?[25]

The failure to date of member countries to successfully conclude the Uruguay Round of the General Agreement on Tariffs and Trade (GATT)—of which Brazil is a founding member—leaves the field wide open for speculation about the future of world trade. For example, continued multilateralism would reflect political pluralism and a free market philosophy. Further fragmentation, on the other hand, could lead to the formation of more mega-blocs. Also, the character of these trading groups can be either open or closed. Europe '92, for instance, could become a major player in world trade or an introspective "Fortress Europe." Although the major challenge to Brazil's economic reconstruction and renewed growth lies at home, a fragmentation of world trade into mega-blocs could have devastating results in the long run. Such a trend could potentially exclude Brazil—and all South America—from the main flows of commerce. Recent signs that the major players in the Uruguay Round are finally approaching an agreement are most welcome news.

As the European Community approaches economic unification, other Western and Central European countries are moving toward applying for membership. Almost all of Africa already has preferential access to the EC market through the Lomé agreements. In North America, the United States, Canada, and Mexico are negotiating a free-trade agreement. More than two-thirds of Mexican exports go to the U.S. market, compared to less than a quarter of Brazil's exports. Central America and the Caribbean, already favored by the Caribbean Basin Initiative, are also moving toward closer regional ties. Finally, Japan, although not ready to admit it, is weaving a trade and investment network encompassing the four tigers, the members of the Association of South East Asian Nations (ASEAN),[26] Australia, and New Zealand.

This trade architecture points toward a tripolar world, led by the EC, the United States, and Japan. The role of South America in this configuration is problematic. Moreover, some analysts consider a tripolar configuration intrinsically unstable, remembering the lessons of history and game theory.[27]

Still other analysts, following the Soviet Empire's collapse, speak of the unipolar moment, a kind of Pax Americana dominated by the United States.[28] The decisive victory in the Gulf war reinforces this perception. This view, however, probably gives too great a weight to the military-political dimension of the international power structure, and too little to the continued strengthening of economic multipolarity.

MERCOSUL* and the Enterprise for the Americas Initiative

While large movements just beginning to unfold may reconfigure world trade, two important concentric initiatives are taking place nearer home. The first is the treaty—signed in March 1991 by the presidents of Argentina, Brazil, Paraguay, and Uruguay—establishing a Southern Cone Common Market by December 31, 1994. This trade unit will encompass 187 million people, a total GDP of $437 billion ($118 billion in industrial products), and an aggregate debt of some $182 billion. These four countries would generate a yearly trade surplus of more than $22 billion.[29]

This subregional common market, to be known as MERCOSUL, will supersede ambitious but unrealistic earlier attempts to create a common market throughout Latin America and the Caribbean. MERCOSUL will benefit from existing trends; Brazil is already the main market for exports from Argentina, Paraguay, and Uruguay.

MERCOSUL is not, of course, a substitute for worldwide trade groups like the GATT. It is, however, a valuable tool for helping the region to better compete internationally by expanding economies of scale, improving allocation of resources, and stimulating regional productivity.

A first instance of common action was the MERCOSUL nations' negotiation with the United States of a Trade and Investment Framework Agreement. Known as the "Rose Garden Agreement" and signed in June 1991 in the presence of presidents Bush and Collor, the framework falls within the scope of the other new hemispheric trade undertaking—the Enterprise for the Americas Initiative.

---

*The Portuguese spelling of MERCOSUR.

Launched in June 1990 by President Bush, this initiative introduced some important ideas:

▲ the long-term goal of a free-trade zone encompassing not just Latin America but the whole hemisphere;

▲ the acknowledgment of the intimate relationship between trade, debt, and investment;

▲ the recognition of the usefulness of subregional common markets or free-trade areas as building blocks leading to hemisphere-wide free trade;

▲ the possibility of reducing the official debt owed by heavily indebted middle-income countries (the concept had already been applied to less developed countries).

Brazil welcomed the Enterprise for the Americas as the most significant U.S. initiative toward Latin America since John F. Kennedy's Alliance for Progress in 1961. It is incumbent on all countries in the hemisphere to transform this vision into a concrete and fruitful reality.

Whither Brazil?

The problems haunting Brazil's future refuse to go away. Indeed, their complexity and interrelatedness look even more formidable now than they did six years ago. A world recession of unknown length and depth, and continuing structural imbalances in the world economy make overcoming the problems only harder.

Nonetheless, we have come a long way. Opportunities—domestic and international—still outweigh the challenges. Brazil has entered a new stage of full democracy that presents it with the opportunity to gather the widest possible support for an ambitious effort of national reconstruction. This was evident when 35 million people, 53 percent of the electorate, chose a young and dynamic leader who had run on a platform of modernization, trade liberalization, market economies, and internationalism.[30]

Despite sometimes wavering congressional support and the fragility of the Brazilian party system, many of President Collor's structural reforms have been approved by Congress. From privatization to trade liberalization, from administrative reforms to a reduced governmental role in the economy, from deregulation to the auction and sale of government assets, from a new understanding between capital and labor to the elimination of protection in the informatics market, a redefined state and a freer market economy are building a new relationship.

In addition, Congress recently passed important measures to assure fiscal balance at all government levels. Noteworthy are a tax reform that will yield a 3 percent public sector surplus in 1992 and legislation to restructure, on feasible but rigorous terms, the debt owed by states and municipalities to the central government.

From right to left across the political spectrum, Brazil's economic thinkers concur on the need to integrate the country competitively into the world economy and to abandon the old state-driven, debt-financed, import substitution model. Those basic reforms, added to Brazil's human and natural endowments, should provide the basis for a jump into modernity.

Notes

1. See Marcílio Marques Moreira, *The Brazilian Quandary*, A Twentieth Century Fund Paper (New York: Priority Press Publications, 1986).

2. Janio Quadros resigned after only seven months in office, opening a political Pandora's box that finally led to the 1964 military takeover and twenty-one years of authoritarian rule.

3. With $116 billion in debt, around $400 billion in GDP in 1990, high inflation, and fast-moving exchange rates, estimating a precise dollar value for GDP is difficult. The ratio of 29 percent compares favorably with most other indebted countries. In contrast, total debt is still almost 3.6 times higher than exports, an indication of the relatively low contribution of Brazilian exports to GDP—only 9 percent.

4. See David D. Hale, "Why Large Government Deficits Cause Inflation in Latin America But Not in the United States," in *Inflation: Are We Next?* ed. Pamela Falk (Boulder, Colo., and London: Lynne Rienner, 1990), pp. 5–33.

5. The reader not familiar with Brazil might believe "cruzeiros" a typographical error. As inflation accelerates, Brazil's currency loses value and changes names: mil-réis, cruzeiros, cruzados, cruzados-novos, cruzeiros.

6. Cf. Fernando Collor, "Mensagem ao Congresso," Brasília: 1991, p. 187.

7. Instituto de Pesquisa Econômica Aplicada (IPEA), Carta de Conjuntura, no. 29, December 1991.

8. Marcílio Marques Moreira, "The Point of View of an Emerging Nation: Brazil," in *Aggressive Unilateralism*, eds. Jagdish Bhagwati and Hugh T. Patrick (Ann Arbor: University of Michigan Press, 1990).

9. The main proponent of this thesis is the "dean" of the Brazilian anthropologists, Gilberto Freire, author of the classic work, *The Masters and the Slaves*. This argument is found in a forceful description of Brazilian history, culture, and reality in Gilberto Freire, *New World in the Tropics: The Culture of Modern Brazil* (New York: Knopf, 1959).

10. The peak may actually have occurred earlier, according to the Instituto Nacional de Pesquisas Espaciais (INPE), *Em Dia*, no. 136, March 1991, p. 1.

11. Cf. Jeremy Bulow and Kenneth Rogoff, "The Buyback Boondoggle," Brookings Papers on Economic Activity, no. 2 (1988), pp. 675–98. On p. 691 the authors discuss "Debt for Do-Good Swaps."

12. Robert B. Reich, *The Work of Nations: Preparing Ourselves for 21st Century Capitalism* (New York: Knopf, 1991), p. 266.

13. Among an ever-broader literature on the subject, see the classic *World Development Report-1980*, (New York: Oxford University Press, 1980) and George Psacheropolous and Ana Maria Arriega, "The Determinants of Early Age Human Capital Formation: Evidence from Brazil," *Economic Development and Cultural Change* 37, no. 4 (July 1989), pp. 683–708.

14. Instituto Brasileiro de Geografia e Estatística (IBGE) and Pesquisa Nacional por Amostra de Domicílios (PNAD), "Síntese de Indicadores da Pesquisa Básica da PNAD de 1981 a 1989," Rio de Janeiro, 1990, pp. 30, 31, and 60.

15. Argentina, with a good education system and, until recently, poor economic performance, is an exception.

16. On the issue of "fair" versus free trade, see Jagdish Bhagwati, *The Rise of Unfair Trade: The World Trading System at Risk* (Princeton, N.J.: Princeton University Press, 1991), pp. 13–22.

17. Peter Evans explores the almost "natural" disputes resulting from the clash between claims of a declining hegemon to retain its challenged superiority and the attempts of newly emerging, assertive traders. The latter are prone to face "a complex combination of private interests and political concerns defined by the core state apparatus," often used "as the vehicle for commercial redress." See "Declining Hegemony and Assertive Industrialization: U.S.-Brazil Conflicts in the Computer Industry," *International Organization* 43, no. 2 (Spring 1989).

18. In May 1991 the government introduced to the Congress a bill proposing complete overhaul of the Law on Industrial Property. It will extend patent protection to all industrial processes and products and introduce improved concepts, rules, and procedures that, together with the already existing copyright legislation, will provide broad, modern, and efficient intellectual property protection. It is expected that the bill will be approved by Congress in the first half of 1992.

19. Upon discovery, Brazil's indigenous peoples were still living in the stone age. Until 1808, in contrast to Spanish America, manufacturing, printing, and institutions of higher learning were not tolerated in Brazil.

20. See Helio Jaguaribe and associates, *Brasil: Reforma ou Caos* (Rio de Janeiro: Paz e Terra, 1989), pp. 29–20.

21. Robert Reich explored the redefinition of the term "national" in *The Work of Nations*, pp. 136–153.

22. A vast literature in books and specialized journals like *Foreign Policy* and *Foreign Affairs* is dedicated to the exploration of this new world economy, awkwardly baptized as the "new international economic order."

23. Brazil's GDP is roughly $400 billion. The eight largest in 1990, excluding China and the then-Soviet Union, are the United States, Japan, Germany, France, Italy, United Kingdom, Canada, and Spain.

24. See, for instance, *Financement et Dette Extérieure des Pays en Developpement* (Paris: Organization for Economic Cooperation and Development, 1991).

25. This subtitle is borrowed from an interesting book on the subject edited by Louis Emmerij, *One World or Several?* (Paris: Development Center, Organization for Economic Cooperation and Development, 1988).

26. Thailand, Malaysia, Indonesia, the Philippines.

27. In a group of three, two of the actors are always tempted to gang up on the third. See C. Fred Bergsten, "The World Economy after the Cold War," *Foreign Affairs* 69, no. 3 (Summer 1990), pp. 102, 103.

28. An outspoken expression of this thesis can be found in Charles Krauthammer, "The Unipolar Moment," *Foreign Affairs* 70, no. 1 (1990/91).

29. The figures are based on data from the Inter-American Development Bank's 1990 *Report on Economic and Social Progress in Latin America* (Baltimore: Johns Hopkins University Press, 1990) and from the IDB's *Annual Report 1990*, Washington, 1991. GNP figures from the *World Bank Atlas-1990* show a total of $455 billion in 1989.

30. This is in stark contrast with the elections in some neighboring countries, where presidents ran on a basic populist platform only to reverse course once in power.

BRAZIL: ECONOMIC STATISTICS

	1986	1987	1988	1989	1990	1991e
Domestic Economy						
Real GDP (index 1985=100)[1]	107.6	111.5	111.4	115.1	110.4	111.7
% change	7.6	3.6	-0.1	3.3	-4.0	1.2
Per capita GDP (US$)[2]	1,810	1,960	2,120	2,540	na	na
Per capita real GDP (% change)[3]	5.8	1.8	-1.7	1.6	-5.9	-0.5
Inflation (% change)[4]	65	416	1,037	1,785	1,467	480
Population (millions)[3]	134.27	136.57	138.91	141.28	143.70	146.15
Unemployment (% of labor force)[1]	3.6	3.7	3.8	3.4	4.0	na
External Economy (US$, millions)						
Exchange rate (cruzeiro-US$)[5]	0.014	0.039	0.264	2.8	67.7	405.0
Merchandise exports[6]	22,349	26,224	33,789	34,383	31,414	31,636
Merchandise imports[6]	-14,044	-15,052	-14,605	-18,263	-20,661	-21,014
Trade balance[6]	8,305	11,172	19,184	16,120	10,753	10,622
Current account balance[6]	-4,856	-818	4,889	1,564	-2,201	863[7]
Total external debt[8]	111,045	121,174	113,469	115,086	121,938	120,132[7]
Total debt service[8]	13,762	9,762	19,377	12,819	8,236	10,063[7]
Reserves excluding gold[8]	5,803	6,299	7,997	8,485	8,238	9,406
Gold reserves (market prices)[8]	957	1,159	1,143	1,194	1,735	757

e estimate
[1] IBGE
[2] World Bank, *World Development Report* estimates
[3] MEFP/SEPE estimates
[4] Conjunto Economico FGV (IGP-DI annual change measured in December)
[5] BACEN/DEPEC–Monthly Bulletin
[6] DECEX/CTIC
[7] January–September 1991
[8] BACEN/DEPEC/DIBAP

8 / U.S. Debt Policy in Latin America: The Melody Lingers on

Benjamin J. Cohen

For the United States, Latin America's decade of debt crisis was a challenge that simply could not be ignored. The crisis began with Mexico's financial collapse in the summer of 1982, and from that moment it was clear that fundamental economic and political interests were at stake. Financial stability, export markets, even hemispheric security arrangements seemed jeopardized by the threat of widespread bankruptcy and default in the region. U.S. officials had no choice but to develop some kind of policy response to the cash flow problems of our southern neighbors.

In fact, Washington's response became the global community's response. The number of actors involved was enormous, including hundreds of private banks and public institutions on the creditor side as well as, on the other side, virtually every country of Latin America and a variety of borrowers elsewhere in the third world. However, while the formal strategy that was quickly implemented to cope with the crisis was conventionally labeled "multilateral," it was in fact largely made in America.

From the start, creditors generally tended to defer to U.S. leadership in dealing with the problems of the so-called middle-income debtors,[1] whose loans had come primarily from private banking sources. This reflected not just the key role of the dollar as the currency of denomination for most commercial bank debt (making the Federal Reserve, in effect, the de facto lender of last resort in the event of a debt-induced financial crisis). More to the point, it reflected the dominant market share of U.S. banks in lending to the troubled middle-income debtors as well as the fact that the most prominent debtors were all located in Latin America, long regarded as Washington's special reserve. It is no accident that the supposedly multilateral strategy was in reality conceived at the Federal Reserve and the Treasury Department. Nor is it any accident that all subsequent major adjustments of the strategy have also emanated from Washington, including in particular the Baker plan of 1985 and the Brady plan of 1989—both named after U.S. Treasury secretaries. There may have been many dancers on the floor, but the melody that was played over the last decade had a distinctly American ring to it.

Today the melody lingers on, still guiding the steps of creditors and debtors. What ideas or themes have impelled its composers, and how successful have their efforts been? Is the tune still in harmony, and, if not, what revisions of the score might be considered?

It is the argument of this chapter that, first and foremost, U.S. debt policy in Latin America has been conditioned by concerns for the financial well-being of America's own lending institutions; in plain words, the main goal was to avert a U.S. banking crisis. By that standard Washington's actions since 1982, through both the Reagan and Bush administrations, must be termed a resounding success. Stability of capital markets has indeed been preserved while at the same time threats to other vital U.S. interests in the region were suppressed. By another standard, however—the financial well-being of Latin America—Washington's achievements to date have regrettably fallen far short of aspirations. Administration officials themselves often proclaimed their goals to include a sustained renewal of development in the debtor nations (frequently referred to as a "return to creditworthiness"). Yet even now, after a decade of tribulation, much of the hemisphere remains mired in stagnation while continuing to labor under the dark shadow of foreign debt. Viewed in this way, U.S. policy is still in urgent need of reform.

The Changing Diagnosis: From Illiquidity to Insolvency

Calls for reform of Washington's strategy are nothing new. Indeed, the melody has already been substantially rewritten twice with the Baker and Brady initiatives. Impressions to the contrary notwithstanding, debt policy reform has not been anathema to the Reagan and Bush administrations. For understandable public relations reasons, officials preferred to project the view that their strategy was robust and working flawlessly; their occasionally thin-skinned sensitivity to adverse comments was not entirely without calculation. In practice, however, they have not been utterly rigid in the face of developing trends.

In fact, three distinct phases may be discerned in the evolution of U.S. debt policy in Latin America. During the first phase, which lasted from the Mexican crisis of August 1982 until introduction of the Baker plan in late 1985, the central emphasis was on rescheduling existing obligations to ease the severe cash flow strains on borrowing nations. In return, debtors were expected to comply with strict programs of domestic "stabilization" sponsored or monitored by the International Monetary Fund (IMF) as well as, of course, to maintain the flow of scheduled interest payments to creditors. The premise of the policy was that borrowers were effectively illiquid rather than in any sense insolvent; that is, whatever the severity of the squeeze on their external payment obligations, their longer-term ability to service debt was fundamentally sound. All they really needed, they were assured, was sufficient time for internal policy adjustments to reignite their stalled development process. With perseverance, higher levels of output and exports would gradually shrink the relative weight of outstanding debt burdens and would even spark some "spontaneous" new foreign financing. Eventually, full readmission to the international capital markets could be hoped for.

Unfortunately, perseverance turned out to be less rewarding than debtors were led to expect. After two years of sharp recession, economic performance did turn upward moderately in 1984. But much of Latin America's trade improvement that year could be directly attributed to the unusually high growth rate in the United States generated by President Reagan's tax cuts, which together with the swollen value of the dollar at the time generated an enormous appetite for imports on the part of American consumers. By 1985, as the U.S. economy cooled off once again, it had become clear that little real progress was actually being made. While budgetary austerity prevailed in most debtor countries, domestic development, it seemed to many, was being retarded or even postponed indefinitely for the sake of preserving creditworthiness in foreign capital markets. Yet despite determined efforts to honor outstanding obligations, very little new money (apart from so-called concerted lending arranged in connection with some IMF stabilization programs) could be drawn forth from private sources.

Capital-hungry debtors were increasingly frustrated with a strategy that resulted not in new financing from abroad but rather the reverse—net resource transfers outward to creditor countries and their banks.

Washington's response, ultimately, was the Baker plan introduced at the IMF/World Bank annual meeting in October 1985. The central aim of the plan, according to then Treasury Secretary James Baker, was to "strengthen" Washington's strategy by supporting more growth-oriented policies in debtor countries as an alternative to the prolonged austerity of previous years. The key was to be some $20 billion of new commercial bank lending over three years to fifteen large middle-income debtors (eleven of them in Latin America), representing an annual increase in overall bank exposure of 2.5 percent. In addition, the World Bank and regional development banks were to kick in an extra $9 billion, representing a 50 percent increase over previous annual totals. The problem was still viewed as one of illiquidity rather than insolvency: given enough time, borrowers were still expected to be able one day to make good fully on their obligations. The purpose of the Baker plan was simply to help jump-start the long-delayed process of recovery.

Regrettably, this phase of policy, which lasted until introduction of the Brady plan in early 1989, also proved a disappointment—and not only because it failed to trigger the substantial increase of private bank lending that Secretary Baker had called for. Even more fundamentally, it failed to promote any significant recovery of debtor economies, as more and more countries found themselves in what one well-informed observer called a "low-growth, high-debt-service trap."[2] The main impact of the prevailing strategy, it became increasingly evident, was to discourage investment in debtor nations, thereby depriving them of the very means they needed—an expansion of productive capacity—to help them earn their way out of their difficulties. In macroeconomic terms, the obligation to maintain full debt service required a corresponding reduction of domestic expenditures in order to release real resources for transfer abroad; in budgetary terms, it required extra public revenues in order to pay the interest on the foreign debt. Both spending cuts and tax increases tended to fall especially hard on domestic capital formation. Yet without capital formation how could debtor countries ever be expected to make good on their obligations? Clearly there was more here than just a temporary squeeze on cash flow.

Gradually, even some administration officials began to acknowledge that for at least some borrowers, the problem really was something a little more like insolvency than mere illiquidity. Commercial debt burdens in some instances were too great and would have to be scaled back in some way. Debt reduction became the new name of the game. As early as 1987, this tactical shift was effectively enshrined in the Treasury's so-called menu approach, newly developed to combat growing creditor weariness with seemingly interminable debt negotiations. The idea was to promote a variety of innovative variations on the standard theme of debt rescheduling. No more simply the plain-vanilla option of postponing maturities on existing bank loans, officials declared. Now lenders should be offered a smorgasbord of imaginative new flavors to entice their continued cooperation. In particular, these might include novel schemes of debt conversion such as debt-for-equity swaps or exchanges for other forms of debt (for example, long-term bonds).

Initially, the approach was intended as little more than a procedural reform to help facilitate the bargaining process between debtors and their commercial creditors. Only the form of obligations was supposed to be altered; the present value of creditor claims would remain largely unchanged. But very soon it became clear that innovations on such a limited scale would still not be enough. Debt reduction, officials were reluctantly forced to conclude, would also have to encompass elements of debt relief (relief being understood to entail measures that effectively reduce not only the nominal stock of conventional debt in the present but also the discounted value of total contractual obligations in the future). Otherwise, debtors would still be hard-pressed to escape the low-growth, high-debt-service trap. The point was finally conceded publicly by the incoming Bush administration in March 1989 with announcement of the Brady plan, urging banks to agree to debt forgiveness or debt service reductions, or both, for selected borrowers in return for various forms of financial support from the IMF and World Bank or creditor governments. And it was confirmed again in June 1990 with proclamation of President Bush's Enterprise for the Americas Initiative, which, in addition to offering regional governments preferential trade benefits and financial backing for market-based economic reforms, promised a negotiated reduction of more than half of Washington's own loans in Latin America. At last the effective insolvency of many of the hemisphere's borrowers was openly admitted at the highest levels of the U.S. government. U.S. debt policy had certainly come a long way!

Making the World Safe for American Banks

To many observers, Washington's successive policy adjustments had an air of improvisation about them: not a strategy at all but rather little more than a series of piecemeal, ad hoc responses to the rush of passing events. "Muddling through" was one of the more charitable phrases used to describe the actions of the Reagan and Bush administrations. But such an interpretation grossly underestimates the ingenuity of the officials most directly involved. In fact, policymakers were extraordinarily successful in terms of their own most fundamental objective—quite simply, to avert a crash of the banking system. No one wanted to repeat the disasters of the 1930s.

Concern was not misplaced: commercial lending in Latin America in the 1970s had accelerated at a dizzying pace, raising bank-exposure levels, as measured by standard capital-asset ratios, to unprecedented heights. By 1982, total debt in the region had swollen to some $315 billion—a fourfold increase in just seven years—of which more than two-thirds was owed to banks. Obligations to U.S. banks alone amounted to some $82.5 billion, equal to one-quarter of all U.S. bank claims overseas. Nearly two-thirds of this was accounted for by just the nine largest American banks, whose overall Latin exposure at the time amounted to more than twice their outstanding capital. (Exposure to the three largest Latin borrowers alone—Argentina, Brazil, and Mexico—added up to more than 135 percent of their capital.) The sense of vulnerability was unmistakable. Major banking institutions were teetering on the brink of bankruptcy. Had default occurred, the stability of the entire American financial system might have been put at risk.

Under the circumstances, U.S. policymakers felt they had no choice. Time had to be bought to lower lenders' high degree of vulnerability; balance sheets had to be protected until levels of exposure, at least in relative terms, could be sufficiently reduced. Most urgently, debtors had to be dissuaded from any temptation to repudiate or otherwise abrogate their full contractual obligations; no form of default, however "conciliatory,"[3] could be even contemplated. Interest payments had to be maintained at full flow in order to help banks avoid any forced write-offs or forgiveness of outstanding claims. The first order of business, quite clearly, was to preserve financial market stability at least cost to lending institutions themselves—a strategy of "containment," as investment banker Pedro-Pablo Kuczynski described it.[4] Can anyone doubt that Washington's goal was successfully attained?

Certainly banks were given enough time to reduce the level of their exposure. By the end of the decade this had dropped to well within the range of the manageable. Vulnerability was lowered in part by a gradual decrease of outstanding claims but mostly by a sharp increase of loan-loss reserves intended to help guard against future disruptions of debt service. Provisions by U.S. banks rose from a derisory 5 percent of aggregate claims on developing countries in 1986 to an average of about 50 percent as of June 1990. By 1991, capital-asset ratios were on average more than double what they had been in 1982. Commercial banking institutions may still have problems today, including deteriorating real estate portfolios and loans for so-called highly leveraged transactions, but there is no longer any serious threat to their continued safety and solvency from the direction of Latin America.

At the same time, direct costs to banks were kept to a minimum. Prior to the Brady plan, remarkably few outright concessions were demanded of the banking community to help cope with the crisis, apart from the frequent rescheduling of maturities as they came due, occasionally accompanied by limited amounts of new lending or modest reductions of interest margins. True, sizable losses did have to be recorded in bank income statements when reserve provisions were increased. But these were paper losses only, no more than bookkeeping formalities, costing nothing at all to the balance sheet unless or until such time as claims might actually be written down, converted at a discount, or forgiven. In practice, only a few smaller institutions voluntarily accepted losses in this way. Most, to the contrary, preferred for as long as possible to hold debtors to their full contractual obligations while continuing to carry claims on their books at 100 percent of face value. Comparatively few real "hits" were ever incurred by banks until the Brady plan came along.

Significantly, something like the Brady plan could not even gain serious attention from the U.S. government until policymakers were persuaded that banks generally were out of the woods on their Latin debt. Only then was Washington willing to consider pushing lenders to bear a greater share of the burden of adjustment to the crisis. Under the Brady plan, formal debt reduction agreements have been negotiated with several key regional borrowers—including, most notably, Mexico, Costa Rica, Uruguay, and Venezuela—and these accords, along with an earlier, essentially similar program for Bolivia, have indeed entailed sizable concessions by banks. In the Mexican and Venezuelan agreements, this mainly meant exchanging existing loans for long-term bonds with reduced face value or interest rates, or possibly both; for Bolivia, Costa Rica, and Uruguay, it principally involved buybacks of outstanding credits at deep discount. Even in these instances, however, the pain has been readily tolerable. Indeed, in each case it may be reasonably argued that the quantitative shrinking of banks' balance sheets was at least partially compensated by a qualitative improvement of the claims remaining in their portfolios. Banks remain the favored child of U.S. policy.

This should not come as any surprise, given the characteristic distribution of policy assignments in the American government. Within Washington's fragmented structure of authority, primary responsibility for issues relating to middle-income borrowers was traditionally entrusted to the Treasury and Federal Reserve rather than to the State Department or industry- or trade-related agencies such as the Commerce Department or Trade Representative's Office. This was bound to introduce a noticeable slant to the government's reaction when the Latin crisis broke in 1982, with highest priority naturally accorded to matters of financial health and stability at home rather than diplomatic or commercial considerations abroad. The threat of political disruption or lost export opportunities in the hemisphere may not have been entirely disregarded over the last decade. It was, however, severely discounted. Among the myriad players on the creditor side of the game, none seemed more threatened than the giants of the banking industry. Is it any wonder, then, that Treasury/Federal Reserve policy would be conditioned most directly by concerns for their underlying safety and soundness? It is hardly necessary to invoke some kind of conspiracy theory to account for the tacit alliance that coalesced in this situation between our biggest international lenders and policymakers in Washington. For banks it was, in a very real sense, simply business as usual.

Playing the Game by Washington's Rules

For Latin America, on the other hand, it was anything but business as usual. Inevitably, Washington's containment strategy, with its emphasis on avoiding default at all costs, meant that debtors rather than creditors would endure the greatest share of the burden of adjustment through stunted development and reverse resource transfers. Over the last decade—the "decade of lost growth"—the pain in the region was far from tolerable. Yet remarkably, debtors, with few exceptions, continued to play the game by Washington's rules. No matter how hard-pressed, most were careful to preserve their lines of communication with other major players and, as much as possible, to abide by the results of negotiations with their creditors, however unfavorable. Economist Rudiger Dornbusch has likened the outcome to a mugging.[5] If so, debtors collaborated fully with their muggers. This too must be considered a measure of the success of U.S. policy.

How was this collaboration achieved? The key was politics: the effectiveness of the U.S.-led strategy was a direct function of fundamental power relationships at both the domestic and international levels. Within debtor countries, a policy of collaboration with creditors tended to correspond most closely to (or conflict least sharply with) the interests of dominant political elites. Throughout the decade, the heaviest burden of adjustment in Latin America fell on precisely those groups that were least well positioned to influence the course of national government—unorganized laborers, peasant farmers, small businessmen, low-ranking civil servants, and urban or rural marginals. Such constituencies lacked the options available to more powerful domestic interests. Private industrialists, large landowners, managers of parastatal enterprises, and the military could often use their influential voices to extract special treatment—exemption from taxation or respite from repressive economic policies. Many were also able, in extremis, to take their movable assets elsewhere—otherwise known as capital flight. Local elites may not have liked the game as it was being played. But the more they could successfully evade the pain of austerity for themselves, the less inclined they were to put pressure on their governments to seek any change of the rules.

At the same time, at the international level, firm pressure was being applied by creditors to avoid any change of the rules, largely through skillful exploitation of the considerable potential for side payments or sanctions inherent in the crisis to shape incentives for debtors. Compliance was encouraged by holding out the prospect of more generous rescheduling terms (longer grace periods, lower interest margins, relaxed policy conditions) and perhaps even some new financing somewhere down the road. Default, conciliatory or otherwise, was discouraged by implicit or explicit threats of direct retaliation. Penalties, debtors were made to understand, might include not just a cessation of medium- or long-term lending or an interruption of short-term trade credits but also a seizure of exports or even the attachment of a debtor's foreign assets, such as commercial airliners, ships, and bank accounts. In Mexico in 1982, as Joseph Kraft has told us, Washington used the offer of emergency assistance quite effectively to strengthen the hand of those in the Mexican government who were opposed to outright default, an option then under serious consideration.[6] By the middle of the decade, it was already quite common to see various kinds of carrots, including multiyear reschedulings or liberalized terms, being dangled before debtor countries as a reward for good behavior, while the stick of tough bargaining (or, looming in the background, the prospect of damaging punishments) was held over the heads of stubborn recalcitrants. Few debtors seemed able to resist these tactics of bribery and coercion.

In short, realpolitik ruled. While domestic politics made it easier for most debtor governments to eschew default, the international influence of creditors reinforced rational fears of potential consequences. Effectively, underlying configurations of power at home and abroad intersected to make collaboration appear by far the least-cost choice for policymakers. Frustrated though they may have been by the skewed distribution of adjustment burdens, debtor governments felt they had little choice but to comply.

Of course, debtors were not without resources of their own in the power game with creditors. They too had some room to shape incentives with side payments or sanctions. Lenders could be tempted into concessions—for example, with such carrots as generous debt-equity conversion programs or improved access to domestic lending markets. Or they could be threatened with the stick of conciliatory default in some form, such as temporary postponement of amortization or a full or partial moratorium on interest payments. But here a problem of collective action intervened: debtors were never able to counter the cohesion of the creditor side with a comparable degree of solidarity of their own. Few borrowing countries had the means to bargain from strength unilaterally. For most, the only possibility would have been to form some kind of common front—some variant of the long-dreaded debtors' cartel—in order to tip the balance of power in their favor. In principle, the notion of debtor solidarity was repeatedly endorsed by the governments of Latin America. In practice, however, effective coordination proved frustratingly elusive.

To some extent, debtors had no one to blame but themselves. Rhetoric notwithstanding, Latin governments have rarely shown much taste for sustained cooperation on issues of this kind. Most of the time, they seem to feel more comfortable simply striking out on their own to negotiate the best possible deals for themselves. But at least as important were the tactics of creditors—particularly their insistence on dealing with debt problems on a "case-by-case" basis, enabling them to take advantage of the unilateralist impulses of debtors. In effect, containment was pursued through a policy of "divide and rule," exploiting differences in the timing of individual financial crises, strategic relationships, domestic political systems, and even the personalities and values of key decisionmakers to obscure debtors' common interests. The designers of containment knew that their terms would be most readily achieved if debtor solidarity could be prevented. Can anyone doubt that this goal too was successfully attained?

Mexico as Test Case: From Rescheduling to Restructuring

Eventually, more attention came to be paid to the interests of debtors, first with the Baker plan's call for additional lending and then with the Bush administration's offers of debt relief under the Brady plan and the Enterprise for the Americas Initiative. Despite the remarkable effectiveness of the containment strategy—or because of it—U.S. policy gradually retreated from its early, virtually exclusive preoccupation with the risks of a financial crash. As bank vulnerability receded, interests other than those of our largest lending institutions began to play a more prominent role in official thinking.

To some extent, the evolution of U.S. policy could be attributed to a growing appreciation of the intractable logic of the low-growth, high-debt-service trap. The case for a reformed strategy of cooperative debt forgiveness, best expressed in economist Paul Krugman's "debt-relief Laffer curve,"[7] gained increasing intellectual respectability. In any event, the de facto insolvency of many borrowing countries became harder to deny as more and more governments simply ceased meeting their interest obligations or fell into serious arrears in order to save valuable foreign exchange. In 1985, Peru under its new president Alan García set a limit on the share of its export revenues that would be set aside for debt service; in 1987, Brazil unilaterally declared a total moratorium on interest transfers to banks. By 1988, more than half of the nations of Latin America were behind in their payments to some degree.

Administration officials were not incapable of learning from experience. Nor were they entirely insensitive to diplomatic or commercial considerations, even if for a long time they were inclined to discount them severely. As interest arrears became more widespread, policymakers were bound to concern themselves with possible threats of political disruption or lost export opportunities for American business. Understandably, administration officials were most apt to change their tune if the health or stability of the United States itself seemed directly at risk. In this respect, not all debtors mattered equally. Administration responses tended to be shaped most by the difficulties of the largest and nearest of the middle-income borrowers, those with the capacity to do real harm to our economy or security arrangements. Above all, it meant that policymakers were influenced by the tribulations of one country in particular: Mexico, our sizable neighbor to the south.

Not only was Mexico, along with Brazil, one of the two biggest debtors in the region, capable by itself of wreaking havoc on the balance sheet of numerous American banks, the country had also become one of our biggest trading partners, and people as well as goods flowed in ever-greater numbers across the common border. At stake whenever the Mexican economy got in trouble were hundreds of thousands of U.S. export jobs and possibly millions of desperately poor illegal immigrants in search of a new life in the United States. No administration could ignore the risks of economic or political destabilization across our long southern frontier. Mexico thus became the principal arena in which our debt policy was forged. Starting with its financial collapse in 1982, Mexico repeatedly acted as the trigger for a revision of thinking in Washington—emerging, in effect, as the test case for determining how the needs of other debtors might be handled. Each phase of the U.S.-led containment strategy had its origins in efforts to cope with significant new developments in the Mexican economy.

The central features of the first phase, for example, stressing temporary liquidity needs, were a direct reflection of the terms of the rescue package worked out for Mexico in August 1982.[8] Official loans totaling some $3.5 billion (plus advance payments for future oil exports) were pledged to enable the Mexicans to avert a debt moratorium, in return for a commitment to negotiate both a stabilization program with the IMF and a rescheduling agreement with commercial creditors. Debt service, in the meantime, was to continue uninterrupted. The perspective was essentially short-term, even though the roots of the crisis went back to the oil boom of the 1970s: flush with export revenues and blessed with abundant reserves of "black gold," Mexico had been considered by lenders to be among the very best of credit risks; the easy availability of foreign finance, in turn, was allowed to distort domestic policies severely, leading to swollen fiscal deficits, excessive monetary growth, and a severely overvalued exchange rate. Since the payments emergency of 1982 was a direct result of the collapse of oil prices that began in mid-1981, one might have thought that something more than a passing liquidity squeeze was at issue. Yet Washington insisted that Mexico's ability to service its $85 billion debt remained fundamentally unimpaired. Once developed, the same formula was subsequently applied to other debtors as well—many with earning prospects even less promising than Mexico's.

The Baker plan was also a response, first and foremost, to the renewed troubles of our southern neighbor. After some modest improvements in 1984, Mexico's performance again began to deteriorate by early 1985, owing not only to the cooling off of the U.S. economy—the main market for Mexican exports—but, even more important, to the continuing decline of world oil prices, which both depressed export revenues and enlarged the public-sector deficit. (Oil at the time accounted for more than two-thirds of Mexican exports and for some two-fifths of fiscal revenues.) By mid-1985, it was clear that, despite heroic efforts by the Mexican authorities to play the game by Washington's rules, the risk of a repeat of 1982's financial collapse was growing.[9] For diplomatic reasons, the Baker Plan called for additional lending to as many as fifteen middle-income debtors, including four countries outside our traditional sphere of interest in Latin America. But few doubted that the main stimulus and intended beneficiary was Mexico. The first major bank rescheduling negotiated following the plan's introduction, a massive $44 billion consolidation initialed in September 1986, was on Mexico's behalf. Including new credits of almost $7.5 billion as well as moderately reduced interest margins, the agreement quickly became the model for other negotiations to follow, though not all debtors could dare hope to replicate Mexico's success in extracting fresh financing from the banks.

Few doubted that Mexico was the primary beneficiary of the Bush administration's policy moves as well, including both the Brady plan and the Enterprise for the Americas Initiative. By 1988, a presidential election year in Mexico, the costs of the country's external debt burden—now in excess of $110 billion—had become patently evident. Starting in mid-1985, the government of President Miguel de la Madrid had committed itself to a comprehensive program of dramatic structural reforms, including not only stringent new budgetary controls but also extensive measures toward domestic deregulation and trade liberalization designed to promote competitive forces in the Mexican economy. Yet growth remained elusive and living standards continued to decline while debt service payments mounted ever higher with each passing year. To many Mexicans, it seemed obvious that good relations with creditors were being purchased with resources that might otherwise have been invested at home. During the 1988 presidential campaign, the low-growth, high-debt-service trap became a central political issue, prompting the eventual winner, establishment candidate Carlos Salinas de Gortari (who as finance minister had been one of the architects of the de la Madrid reform program), to make debt reform one of the main planks of his platform.

The Brady plan offered public-sector support for negotiated reductions of private commercial liabilities. As before, the first major agreement under the new approach, worked out over the summer of 1989, was with Mexico—a complex package of discounted debt conversions effectively reducing the country's interest payments to banks by about one-third. In line with precedent, the Mexican agreement quickly became the model for accords that followed with Costa Rica, Venezuela, and others. In its Enterprise for the Americas Initiative, the administration placed a heavy emphasis on preferential trade benefits and market-based reforms as the key to renewed growth in the hemisphere. Once again, the approach is being tested first in the current free trade negotiations with Mexico. A decade after the Latin debt crisis began, Mexico remains the bellwether of U.S. policy in the region.

Shifting the Burden of Adjustment

As in the Sherlock Holmes story, then, the key to the plot lies in what did not happen—the dog that didn't bark. The banking system did not crash; most debtors did not formally default; threats of political disruption or lost export opportunities in the hemisphere were effectively minimized; and Mexico was not destabilized. The extent to which U.S. policy realized all its principal objectives is not fully appreciated. But at what price were these goals achieved? For banks, as indicated earlier, the pain has been slight, even taking into account the concessions that have so far been negotiated under the aegis of the Brady plan. The burden of adjustment has fallen disproportionately not only on debtors but on the taxpayers of the United States and other creditor nations as well. These implications of Washington's containment strategy have not been fully appreciated either.

For much of Latin America, a renewal of sustained development still seems exasperatingly beyond reach. Among the dozen regional borrowers classified by the World Bank as "severely indebted" in the 1980s, only two—Chile and Costa Rica—have as yet been able to improve performance sufficiently to be graduated to the ranks of the merely "moderately indebted." In a recent survey of Latin America and the Caribbean by the Institute of International Economics, only five countries could be labeled "growing" by the end of the decade (Barbados, Chile, Colombia, Costa Rica, and Paraguay), compared with eleven that were identified still as "stagnating" and five as "declining."[10] And in 1990, according to the World Bank's most recent annual report, per capita incomes in Latin America continued to drop on average by some 2.6 percent—the poorest showing of any region of the third world. Although growth did return to parts of the hemisphere in 1991, for most countries expansion has remained uncertain at best.

Not even the few direct beneficiaries of the Brady plan have had all that much to boast about. Commercial bank loans have been effectively reduced, but new liabilities were created to replace them. On a net basis, the shrinkage of nominal claims under the region's first four Brady agreements has amounted to less than $12 billion overall. In present value terms, the savings appear substantial, ranging from an estimated 23 percent of the face value of Venezuela's restructured bank debt to 31 percent for Mexico and to as much as 77 percent in the case of Costa Rica. But in terms of current cash flow, relief so far has been quite modest, ranging from an estimated $1.8 billion a year for Mexico to no more than $460 million for Venezuela. Expressed as a percentage of projected exports, cash flow savings vary from some 6 percent for Mexico to no more than 2.5 percent for Venezuela.[11] In reality, the concessions extracted from banks to date have been something less than munificent.

In the United States and other creditor nations, meanwhile, an increasing share of the burden of adjustment has been shifted toward taxpayers quietly, without the benefit of much public debate. Most evident are the budgetary impacts of official debt cancellations like those proposed under the Enterprise for the Americas Initiative: the counterpart of any cash flow savings for debtors is a loss of domestic public receipts that over time must be matched, if expenditures are not to be reduced, by offsetting increases of fiscal revenues from other sources. Less obviously, Washington's containment strategy has functioned to transfer a growing portion of the risk and exposure in lending to middle-income debtors incrementally from commercial lenders to creditor governments and multilateral agencies like the World Bank and IMF. While bank claims on middle-income debtors have been declining, obligations to official creditors have more than tripled since the crisis began.[12]

In part, this trend reflects continued lending along traditional lines by the governments of capital market countries as well as by the World Bank and IMF (whose claims, of course, are backed primarily by those same financial powers). Less traditionally, it reflects the impact of the Brady plan's emphasis on public support of debt forgiveness or debt service reduction by the private sector. Since 1989 more than $6 billion of government money has been provided to facilitate Brady plan negotiations, either to assist in direct buybacks of bank debt or to collateralize the principal or "enhance" (that is, guarantee) interest payments on newly created obligations. As a result of these developments, official debt service paid by middle-income debtors has nearly doubled, from 5.2 percent of exports in 1982 to 9.7 percent in 1989, even as the ratio of private debt service to exports fell by nearly half, from 27.2 percent to 16.5 percent.[13] Increasingly, it is the governments of the creditor nations—and, through them, their taxpayers—rather than commercial lenders who are becoming the most vulnerable to the difficulties of borrowers in Latin America or elsewhere.

This burden shifting has come to pass so swiftly in large measure because public interest in the debt crisis as such has drained away as the threat of a banking crash has receded. Back in 1982, observers were riveted by possible scenarios of financial collapse or global depression. For most bystanders the importance of the debtors lay not in themselves but rather in what their travails might mean for creditors. Latin America has always struggled with poverty, after all; nothing new or exciting in that. The real story, it appeared, lay in the travails of lenders. As time passed, however, and bank vulnerability was gradually reduced, the troubles of debtors came to seem less exciting than merely tedious, and attention has understandably been diverted to more gripping events elsewhere, such as the recent anti-Communist revolutions in Eastern Europe and the Soviet Union. As a result, perceptions of the Latin debt problem have grown more benign, despite the lingering difficulties of debtors and growing costs for taxpayers. If disaster is no longer a threat, why worry?

Toward a Better Solution

The answer, plainly, is that worry is still justified so long as Latin America continues to struggle under the shadow of the debt. Administration officials may prefer to cultivate the view that the crisis is largely over; certainly such a perception helps avoid challenge to the still-high priority accorded private creditor interests under the containment strategy. But the traditional approach is not the only one possible, nor does it necessarily best serve the broader national interests of the United States. At a minimum, renewed public debate should be promoted to review priorities and consider alternatives. More to the point, we might seriously ask whether we as taxpayers really approve of the present distribution of adjustment costs. Policy reform should not be excluded by default (pardon the pun).

A strong case can be made for liberalizing the modest elements of relief currently available to Latin borrowers under the Brady plan and the Enterprise for the Americas Initiative—moving policy, in effect, a few more steps along the evolutionary path already evident since 1982. The challenge today is not at the level of principle: after years of denial, administration officials have effectively acknowledged the de facto insolvency of many of the hemisphere's debtors. The issue, rather, lies at the level of practice—the limited scale of tangible benefits so far offered to help debtors achieve that coveted "return to creditworthiness." It is clear that much of the region remains caught in the low-growth, high-debt-service trap, still unable to make good fully on its foreign obligations. Thus it should also be clear that more help is needed if development is to be renewed on a truly sustained basis. It is no longer a question of diagnosis. Now we are just dickering about the price.

Should we be prepared to pay a higher price? Surely our interest in a healthier Latin America requires little demonstration. Who can doubt that over the long term, our destiny as a nation is closely linked to the fortunes of our hemispheric neighbors? This is more than just a matter of commercial opportunities or the risk of illegal immigration. More broadly, our national security is at stake should the threat of economic or political instability be allowed to fester on our doorstep. The real question is whether we can afford not to do more to relieve debt burdens in the region.

If debtors are to bear a smaller share of the costs of adjustment, someone else will have to pick up the tab. Should this be taxpayers, who have already been obliged to assume a growing portion of outstanding risk and exposure in Latin America? Or should this be the banks, whose concessions to date have been more impressive in appearance than substance? Equity as well as efficiency considerations would seem to argue for greater sacrifices by creditors. It is the banks, after all, that generated the loans in the first place; the ethics of capitalism place the responsibility for business decisions, good or bad, squarely on those who make them. And now that the vulnerability of creditors has been reduced to manageable proportions, there seems little reason not to expect them to do more to lighten the burdens of debtors. Bankers argue that this is not the time—that the industry today, in the midst of a "double-dip" recession at home, is just too weakened by sagging asset values to offer greater concessions to borrowers abroad. However, this overlooks both the high level of reserves already set aside to cover the cost of Latin debt reductions and the qualitative improvements that could be anticipated in the claims that would remain. Although some institutions might be stretched a bit, the industry as a whole can now surely afford to take a bigger hit.

How might policy reform be designed to persuade banks to face up to the need for much greater relief for Latin borrowers? The techniques of debt relief are familiar, ranging from interest rate reductions to conversions or buybacks at discount to outright forgiveness of existing obligations. No great imagination is needed to expand on the traditional menu of options. But how can we overcome the effective resistance of creditors? As is well known, one of the biggest obstacles to a reformed strategy of cooperative debt forgiveness is the difficulty of organizing effective collective action among the many banks involved. Creditor solidarity was relatively easy to maintain so long as the issue was the behavior of debtors; nothing concentrates the minds of bankers so much as the fear of default on their loans. The challenge of achieving a common front is far more tricky when it is the banks themselves that are expected to make the sacrifices. Even if lenders were all agreed that greater relief was in their common interest, each one individually would still have an incentive to "free ride" on the sacrifices of others—avoiding any share of the costs of concessions while hoping to reap the benefit of any ensuing gain in the value of their own claims. Ideally, this obstacle might be overcome through the intervention of a neutral international institution designed specifically for the purpose of facilitating a negotiated resolution of debt difficulties on a mutually beneficial basis; one possible proposal along such lines has been offered elsewhere.[14] Lacking the necessary political consensus for such an approach, however, it seems necessary to continue relying on the leadership of the U.S. government to promote further accommodations by the banking industry. The melody must still be written in Washington.

To date, policymakers have tried first exhortation (the Baker plan) and then financial incentives (the Brady plan) to gain the cooperation of banks—with only limited effectiveness. Why not now apply to banks the same forceful tactics of bribery and coercion that were previously directed with such great success toward debtors? If additional public money is to be provided to support Brady plan negotiations, why not make it conditional on much more generous concessions than have been offered until now? And if banks continue to prove recalcitrant, why not threaten them with stiffer penalties for noncooperation? At a minimum, free riders could be warned that they would be subjected to stiffer regulation or prudential supervision. More ambitiously, administration support for industry objectives in any future banking reform legislation could be explicitly tied to a commitment for more liberal terms of relief for debtors. In extremis, officials could even threaten to negotiate settlements directly over the heads of creditors, as was done in the 1940s to clear up an earlier crisis of Latin American debt. Banks still dance to Washington's tune. It is time to brighten up the score.

Notes

1. As defined by the World Bank, middle-income countries are those with a GNP per capita between $580 and $6,000.

2. Anne O. Krueger, "Debt, Capital Flows, and LDC Growth," *American Economic Review* 77, no. 2 (May 1987), p. 163.

3. The apt word is used by Anatole Kaletsky in *The Costs of Default* (New York: Priority Press Publications, 1985).

4. Pedro-Pablo Kuczynski, "The Outlook for Latin American Debt," *Foreign Affairs* 66, no. 1 (Fall 1987), pp. 129–49.

5. Rudiger Dornbusch, "International Debt and Economic Instability," *Federal Reserve Bank of Kansas City Economic Review*, January 1987, p. 15.

6. Kraft, Joseph, *The Mexican Rescue* (New York: Group of Thirty, 1984), p. 2.

7. Devised by analogy with the familiar Laffer curve, which suggests that governments may actually increase tax revenues by reducing tax rates, the debt-relief Laffer curve suggests that creditors may actually increase expected debt service by forgiving part of a country's debt. The logic is that the country's debt stock may have grown to the point where its capacity to service debt is significantly impaired.

8. Kraft, *The Mexican Rescue*.

9. Luis Rubio F. and Francisco Gil-Diaz, *A Mexican Response* (New York: Priority Press Publications, 1987).

10. John Williamson, *The Progress of Policy Reform in Latin America*, Policy Analyses in International Economics, no. 28 (Washington, D.C.: Institute for International Economics, January 1990).

11. International Bank for Reconstruction and Development, *World Debt Tables 1990–91: External Debt of Developing Countries*, vol. 1: *Analysis and Summary Tables* (Washington, D.C.: World Bank, 1990), p. 35.

12. Ibid, p. 10.

13. Ibid, pp. 7, 40.

14. Benjamin J. Cohen, "A Global Chapter 11," *Foreign Policy*, no. 75 (Summer 1989), pp. 124–125.

About the Authors

Robert Bottome is director and partner of the VenEconomía group, made up of financial consultants and various publications, including *VenEconomy Weekly* and *VenEconomy Monthly*. Mr. Bottome is also the Caracas representative of Standard Chartered Bank of London. He is on the board of various Venezuelan companies and is a member of the boards of the Caracas and the British-Venezuelan Chambers of Commerce. A graduate of Williams College, he has spent thirty-four years in brokerage, investment, and financial analysis.

Roberto Bouzas is research fellow at the Latin American School of Social Sciences (FLACSO) and research associate at the National Council on Scientific and Technical Research (CONICET), both in Buenos Aires. He has taught economics in Latin America and the United States and has published widely on international economic issues. He was recently a visiting scholar at Stanford University's Center for Latin American Studies. Mr. Bouzas holds a B.A. from the University of Buenos Aires and a B.A. and M.A. in economics from Cambridge University.

Benjamin J. Cohen is the Louis G. Lancaster Professor of International Political Economy at the University of California, Santa Barbara. He has served as an economist at the Federal Reserve Bank of New York and has held teaching positions at Princeton University and the Fletcher School of Law and Diplomacy at Tufts University. Dr. Cohen was also senior visiting fellow at the Council on Foreign Relations. He has published numerous books on international economic issues, many of which have been translated. He holds a Ph.D. in economics from Columbia University.

Anatole Kaletsky has been economics editor of *The Times* of London since 1990. A onetime columnist for *The Economist*, in 1979 he joined *The Financial Times*, where his positions included Washington correspondent, international economics correspondent, and New York bureau chief. Mr. Kaletsky won a British Press Award in 1980 for his columns on the economic policy of the Thatcher government. A graduate of Cambridge University's King's College, Mr. Kaletsky holds a B.A. in mathematics and a diploma in economics. He also received an M.A. in economics from Harvard University.

Marcílio Marques Moreira is Brazil's minister of economy, finance, and planning. He was Brazil's ambassador to the United States from 1986 to 1991. He has held key positions in the banking industry and at several universities. The author of numerous books and articles, Minister Marques Moreira is a graduate of the Instituto do Rio Branco (Brazil's diplomatic academy), the State University of Rio de Janeiro School of Law, and Georgetown University, where he received an M.A. in political science.

Felipe Ortiz de Zevallos M. is founder and chairman of APOYO, a consulting, publishing, and polling institute in Lima, Peru. He is also an associate professor in economics at the University of the Pacific. He is a member of the consultative council of the Ministry of Foreign Affairs and has served in a similar capacity for the ministries of Economics and Finance; Planning, Energy and Mines; Industry, Tourism, Commerce, and Integration; and Housing and Construction. Mr. Ortiz de Zevallos is the founder and director of the Institute of Economic Development, a graduate school of management. He holds an M.S. in management from the University of Rochester.

Luis Rubio is director general of CIDAC, the Center of Research for Development, an independent think tank devoted to the study of economic and political policy issues in Mexico. Before joining CIDAC, he served as planning director at Citibank in Mexico and as adviser to Mexico's secretary of the treasury. He is a member of the board of directors of Banamex, writes a weekly column for *La Jornada*, and is a regular contributor to *The Washington Post*. Dr. Rubio is the author and editor of sixteen books. His M.A. and Ph.D. in political science are from Brandeis University.

ABOUT THE AUTHORS

Arturo Valenzuela is professor of government and director of the Center for Latin American Studies at Georgetown University. He has been a Danforth Fellow, a Fulbright Scholar, a fellow at the Woodrow Wilson International Center for Scholars, and a visiting scholar at Oxford University, the University of Sussex, the University of Chile, the Catholic University of Chile, and the University of Florence. Most recently, he was professor of political science and director of the Council on Latin American Studies at Duke University. He has published widely; his most recent book, *A Nation of Enemies: Chile Under Pinochet*, was coauthored with Pamela Constable. He holds an M.A. and Ph.D. in comparative politics from Columbia University.